Houdini's "Girl Detective"

The Real-Life Ghost-Busting Adventures of Rose Mackenberg

Compiled and introduced by Tony Wolf

CONTENTS

MISS ROSE MACKENBERG VS. THE SPOOK RACKET...........7

NOTES ON THIS ANTHOLOGY 21

SPIRITUALISM, POSSIBLY TRUE, AND "SPIRITUALISM" DEMONSTRABLY FALSE 23

MYSTIC CAMERAS DUPE GRIEVED (WITH FASCINATING FACTS ABOUT ECTOPLASM)..29

SIX $25 FEES BOUGHT ME SIX LICENSES TO "MARRY AND TO BURY" 39

DWARF INSIDE "PSYCHIC" DRUM CAUSES EXPOSÉ OF MYRA'S MESMERIC MUSIC 49

BLASÉ OLD LONDON PROVES HAPPY HUNTING GROUND FOR SUAVE SEERESSES WHO THRIVE ON CREDULITY 59

INCREDIBLE GRAFT IN THE SALE OF "MAGIC CHARMS, AMULETS AND LOVE PHILTRES" IS REVEALED 67

MANY SPIRITUALISTS CLAIMED HOUDINI HAD POWER TO ENTER FOURTH PLAIN, DISSOLVING MATERIAL BODY 75

MILLIONAIRE "MEDIUM" REJECTS HOUDINI'S $10,000 CHALLENGE THAT HE'LL DUPLICATE "FEATS" BY MAGIC 85

Miss Rose Mackenberg vs. the Spook Racket

by Tony Wolf

"And the stately ships go on
  To their haven under the hill;
But O for the touch of a vanished hand,
  And the sound of a voice that is still!"

- Alfred, Lord Tennyson, "Break Break Break" (1842)

"What? If I told you all about the tricks?
Upon my soul?—the whole truth, and nought else,
And how there's been some falsehood—for your part,
Will you engage to pay my passage out,
And hold your tongue until I'm safe on board?"

- Robert Browning, "Mr. Sludge, The Medium" (1864)

The practice of purportedly communicating with the dead has existed throughout human history, but we can date the Spiritualism movement as such to the activities of the Fox sisters of Hydesville, New York, circa 1848.

Margaret and Kate Fox, both young teenagers, claimed that they were in spiritual communication with an entity named "Mr. Splitfoot" (a nickname for the Christian Devil), who was able to respond to questions by producing clicking or rapping noises. A code was established by which questions could be answered by raps representing the words "yes" and "no"; the raps could also spell out words by indicating letters of the alphabet.

As the sisters' fame grew, a number of investigators quickly concluded that the girls were producing the rapping noises themselves, by clicking or cracking their toe joints to create a sound similar to snapping one's fingers. Nevertheless, their "mediumship" was widely embraced, especially by local members of the Quaker faith, as proof of life beyond death.

Kate and Margaret soon became professional mediums - so-called "sensitives" who were in touch with the spirit world. Managed by their much older sister, Leah, their séances became a popular media sensation. Within a few years, hundreds more people were claiming to be able to communicate with the dearly departed.

In 1888, the adult Margaret and Kate admitted that the mysterious "spirit rappings" that made their early fame and fortune were, indeed, simply mischievous crackings of their toe joints, a technique that Margaret proceeded to publicly demonstrate. Their communion with "Mr. Splitfoot" had been nothing more than a schoolgirl prank that had spiralled out of their control. They also strongly denounced the practice of spiritualism as fraud and delusion; by that time, however, the horse had fled the stable. The Fox sisters had inadvertently inspired an international occult subculture of both true believers and cynical con-artists who elaborated "spirit rapping" into ever more complex and spectacular phenomena.

Popular attempts at communication with the spirit world included the planchette method, in which two or more people would each touch their hands to the surface of a small, wheeled board set up to roll freely across a large sheet of paper. A pencil attached to the board, thus, would leave an impression on the paper, writing words that were held to originate "beyond the veil".

"Table-tipping" séances were also very much in vogue during the mid-late 19th century. A group of people would gather in a dark room and stand or seat themselves about a table, each laying both of their hands upon the table's surface. After impassioned invocations that the supernatural forces should make themselves felt, the table would begin to tremble and shake, then often tip and rock about alarmingly, its feet banging on the floor in apparent answer to questions. The experience left the sitters startled and frequently convinced that some mysterious agency was at work.

Séance attendees were often desperately grieving people who hoped to make contact with the spirits of deceased friends and relatives. Others sought life advice from the Great Beyond, staking major financial, health and other personal decisions on the advice of "spirits", whose validity was seemingly proven by table-tipping and other "physical phenomena" conjured in the séance parlors. All of this, skeptics believed, was a perfect recipe for superstition and exploitation.

As spiritualism prospered and diversified, it also attracted the attention of new generations of skeptical investigators and exposers, concerned that vulnerable people were being deluded and/or defrauded. Scientists and professional magicians were prominent among the protagonists the burgeoning "anti-Spiritualism" movement.

The mysteries of the planchette and of table-tipping, for example, was quickly debunked by scientifically-minded skeptics as an example of the ideomotor effect in action. This curious and little-known but entirely natural phenomenon had first been tested and defined by the English physician and séance-investigator William B. Carpenter in 1852. It essentially described the unconscious influence of imagination and expectation upon muscular activity.

In table-tipping séances, the collective expectation that the table *would* begin to move caused sitters to involuntarily bear down upon its surface, with greater or lesser degrees of muscular force, their combined, uncoordinated efforts inevitably causing the table to shift and rock. As the table genuinely appeared to be moved by an invisible, supernatural power, the sitters' emotional excitement exacerbated their ideomotive responses as they attempted to "follow" the table's erratic actions, thereby creating a semi-coordinated but still involuntary effort that perpetuated and amplified the table's movement.

Skeptics also noted that table-tipping séances could very easily be deliberately manipulated by one or more insincere and mischievous "sitters". Even more spectacular effects - such as levitations - were simple to conjure with basic props, such as wooden slats or strong wire loops strapped to the "medium's" forearms. Invisibly emerging from their sleeves and pressing underneath the tabletop, these devices allowed the unscrupulous "medium" to raise the table while keeping their palms pressed flat to its surface.

Much the same explanation was offered for planchette seances - sincere but naïve sitters fell victim to the subtle, convincing illusions of the ideomotor effect, whereas anyone with a prankish streak could easily create "spirit writings" by taking covert control of the planchette.

Even as simple and rational explanations for séance phenomena were being sought and found, the rapid scientific advances of the late 19th century spurred sporadic, but often deeply serious efforts to apply new technologies to the matter of communication with the souls of the departed. Sir Oliver Lodge, a pioneer in the fields of electromagnetic and radio research, was also a member of the Ghost Society and served as president of the London-based Society for Psychical Research from 1901 to 1903.

Lodge's research into electromagnetism had convinced him that the universe was filled with aether - a hypothetical, and since discredited, light-bearing medium. He believed that the spirit world was to be found in the aether and that the nascent medium of radio might allow communication "between the worlds".

No such appliance was deemed necessary by mediums such as Catherine-Elise Müller, a young French woman who believed that she was in psychic contact with the spirits of an ancient Indian princess, the 17th century occultist Cagliostro, Victor Hugo and Esenale, an inhabitant of the planet Mars. Miss Müller's purported communiqués with Esenale eventually resulted in her transcription of a functional Martian alphabet and language. The phrase "dode ne haudan te meche metiche Astane ke de me veche", for example, translated as "this is the house of the great man Astane, whom thou hast seen."

Skeptics, including the psychologist Théodore Flournoy who worked closely with Müller over a period of about five years, noted that her Martian language was almost identical in structure to her native French. In 1900, Flournoy presented his findings in a book titled *From India to the Planet Mars*, which became a popular curiosity amidst the prevailing cultural debates on spiritualism.

It should be noted that while Flournoy did not believe that Miss Müller was actually communicating with Martians, nor did he think that she was deliberately inventing her Martian visions. Flournoy expressed admiration for his subject's powers of "unconscious imagination" and also protected her identity by giving her the pseudonym "Helene Smith".

The medium herself was not pleased with his book, which presented her as a psychological case study in glossolalia rather than as a psychic; however, *From India to the Planet Mars* made her reputation and she continued to use the Helene Smith pseudonym professionally.

Prior to the First World War, Spiritualism had generally co-existed peacefully alongside mainstream religions. Between 1914-1920, however, the combined tolls of the War and the Spanish Flu pandemic left many millions of people bereaved. The shared eschatological horror of so many lives snuffed out within a short period fostered a massive renaissance of Spiritualism during the 1920s, as grieving relatives hoped to be able to communicate with their lost loved ones.

Many made use of the Ouija board, a commercial development of the old planchette system, re-popularized as a spirit communication medium by people such as Pearl Curran. Curran famously claimed (and may well have believed herself) to be the reincarnated spirit of a 17th century Dorsetshire farm girl named Patience Worth.

Believers held that the sliding of the planchette across the surface of the alphabet board could spell out "spirit messages"; skeptics saw simply another manifestation of the ideomotor effect in action, with the planchette revealing the sitters' own collective, spontaneous and subconscious expectations.

The standard opening question of "is any spirit present?", for example, was typically answered in the affirmative because the sitters collectively wanted and expected the answer to be "yes". Obviously, if no spirit was present then the planchette would not move at all and the experiment would be over, and it would be illogical (or indicative of a spirit with a well-developed sense of irony) for the planchette to move to "no" under these circumstances.

At the follow-up question, "what is your name?", the planchette would typically meander until it came to indicate a single letter - perhaps the letter B - after which, following the conventions of the spelling of names, it would naturally tend to move to one of the five vowel options, such as E. By this point the curious quasi-cooperation of collective expectation via ideomotor action would have taken effect and the name would emerge as Ben, Beatrice,

Betty and so-on. Apparent mistakes, misspellings and non sequiturs were easily overlooked or rationalized as spiritual "interference" or "mischief".

Ouija board and table-tipping séances were typically casual, private affairs, but many others of the new legions of the bereaved attended commercial spiritualist séances staged by professional mediums. Attendees would typically pay a few dollars for the experience of singing hymns, listening to a sermon on the Great Beyond and then sitting with other seekers, either around a table or in pew-like rows of chairs, in a pitch-dark room wherein all manner of apparently supernatural phenomena took place.

Often the medium would be seemingly securely restrained, by being bound hand and foot to a chair, for example, or by having their hands held by "sitters" to either side. Regardless of the restraints, trumpets and other musical instruments apparently hovered and played themselves; mysterious, glowing objects flitted about in the gloom. The séance would invariably culminate in the transmission of purported messages from the dearly departed, often via a "control", or co-operative spirit, who ostensibly spoke to, or even possessed the medium.

Thus, events that would have been considered miraculous, if not actually blasphemous, during the preceding centuries became commonplace within the context of the 1920s séance parlor.

During this post-War boom period, some prominent spiritualists, most notably Sir Arthur Conan Doyle, began to speak seriously in terms of their nascent religion supplanting the more traditional, established faiths.

Sir Arthur's interest in the occult extended back to about the same time he first conceived of Sherlock Holmes, during the late 1880s. The irony of the respected creator of perhaps the world's most famous rational materialist whole-heartedly embracing the cause of spiritualism was not lost on Doyle's contemporaries.

His adamant championing of the so-called Cottingley fairy photographs, for example, attracted widespread media ridicule and did no lasting good to his reputation. Many decades later, those pictures were confirmed as having been faked by the simple expedient of attaching cut-out paper "fairy" figures to hat-pins stuck into the ground. The proven fact of their fakery would not have surprised many commentators during the early 1920s, who struggled to fathom how a man of Doyle's education and worldliness could have been so thoroughly deceived by a pair of imaginative, mischievous schoolgirls.

Doyle wrote in his memoir "Memories and Adventures" that the life of his father, Charles Altamont Doyle, was "full of the tragedy of unfulfilled powers and undeveloped gifts." The elder Doyle suffered badly from alcoholism and depression for many years and spent his later life confined in psychiatric hospitals, producing many whimsical paintings of fairies. Some of Sir Arthur's biographers have speculated that his enthusiasm for the occult - and his impassioned defence of the Cottingley fairies in particular - may also have represented an unconscious wish to redeem his father.

Although Doyle himself vehemently denied it - especially as he rose to prominence as the chief propagandist for Spiritualism - it's very difficult not to at least partly attribute his embrace of that belief to his family's tragic losses during the first two decades of the 20th century. Doyle's wife Louisa had died of pneumonia in 1906. Eight years later his son Kingsley, a soldier who had been wounded at the Somme, succumbed to the same disease, while Doyle's brother Innes, his two brothers-in-law and two nephews all died shortly after the War. Sir Arthur's fellow Spiritualist, Sir Oliver Lodge, also lost his son in the conflict.

Doyle's chief opponent in the burgeoning public debate on spiritualism was the magician and escape artist Harry Houdini. Emerging from very humble beginnings as Ehrich Weiss, the third son of an itinerant rabbi, by the early 1920s Houdini had mastered both stage magic and showmanship to become one of the most famous entertainers in the world. The novel act that secured his reputation was the "challenge escape", in which he would free himself from the most nefariously difficult restraints that could be imagined by locksmiths, industrial manufacturers, jailers and newspaper editors alike.

Houdini's zealotry in exposing the methods of the "spook racketeers", was directly inspired by the death of his beloved mother, Cecilia Weiss, in 1913. His wild grief spurred him to try to contact his mother's spirit via séances with mediums, but of course, as a professional in the art of deception and a former mediumistic huckster himself, he instantly saw through their use of magic tricks and stagecraft. In the secret parlance of the spook racket, Houdini was an "open-eye" - one who was wise to the game - whereas Doyle would have been classified as a "shut-eye", a devout believer.

These distinctions were not, however, as clearly cut as might first appear. Doyle also professed faith in the scientific method and had been unconvinced by the results of some of his own investigations into certain self-styled mediums; he was, in fact, deeply aware of spiritualist charlatanry, regarding it as a base misuse of a noble religious cause. For all that, however, Doyle was both strongly predisposed towards belief in the supernatural and untrained in the mechanisms of deceit, relying instead on his less-then-Holmesian powers of observation and his sense of an individual's character.

Houdini, meanwhile, admitted no enmity against those shut-eye mediums who were sincere in their practice of Spiritualism as a religion - he believed, instead, that such people (and their followers) were simply deluded and prone to fantasy - but he felt contempt for the open-eye "spirit frauds" who profited by perverting the craft of stage magic into a cynical exploitation of the vulnerable and gullible. Indignation mounted into righteous fury and Houdini commenced his own crusade against the spook racket.

Curiously, given their diametrically opposed views on a subject that was of great emotional and intellectual importance to both men, Houdini and Doyle were quite close friends. They first met during the magician's performance engagements in London in 1920, and were, for several years thereafter, frequent correspondents who enjoyed each other's company whenever they were able to meet.

To Houdini's ongoing frustration, however, Doyle was convinced that some of the illusions of stage magic performance were evidence of real supernatural powers. Adhering to the magician's code, Houdini could not explain the mechanics of these tricks to his friend, but he did repeatedly assure Doyle that there was nothing of "unnatural magic" in his performances and that anyone who was skilled in the working of tricks could do as he did.

For his part, Doyle initially supported Houdini's efforts to root out charlatan mediums, for he was well aware that many self-proclaimed Spiritualists were frauds preying on the gullible.

So it was that Houdini and Doyle formed something of a mutual admiration society until, unfortunately but inevitably, their bonds of friendship were shattered during a very public and bitter dispute over the "spiritualist question".

The event that ended their friendship was undertaken with the best of intentions by all concerned. Lady Conan Doyle was an enthusiastic amateur "psychographer", who by all accounts genuinely believed that she could channel the words of spirits through the practice of "automatic writing". During a séance with Houdini she produced a written message ostensibly from Houdini's mother Cecilia, but Houdini, though he remained gracious at the time, was unconvinced. The message consisted largely of generic platitudes; it had also been written in English, a language his mother did not speak, and had been headed with a drawing of a cross, a symbol unlikely to have been used by the devoutly Jewish Cecilia Weiss.

Sir Arthur, however, apparently believing that Houdini had been converted to Spiritualism by this experience, publicly made a statement to that effect, which Houdini was forced to refute; Doyle took that refutation as impugning his wife's honour. So ended a fascinatingly unlikely friendship, as the two men entered a bitter public relations war via the media.

The 1920s, thus, saw the emergence of spiritualism as a major fad in international popular culture, with the true believers finding their champion in Sir Arthur Conan Doyle and Harry Houdini crusading on behalf of the skeptics. Innumerable articles on the subject appeared in newspapers and magazines, while books and lectures, both pro- and anti-, did a flourishing trade.

Notably, a succession of professional magicians, prominently including Howard Thurston, delighted in out-séancing the mediums by producing all manner of phantasmagoric "phenomena" in the context of vaudeville performance. Presented as nothing more nor less than ghostly entertainments, these acts would evolve into the "midnight spook shows" of the 1950s and '60s cinema circuit. The combative Houdini, however, also staged outright exposés, directly challenging the supernaturalism of Spiritualistic staples such as table-tipping and the manifestation of ectoplasm by means of practical demonstration.

The séance also became a reliable staple in Jazz Age fiction, to the extent that the mysterious (and, more often than not, crooked) medium and the rational "ghost buster" became stock characters in the novels, plays and silent films of the period.

One of the most prolific authors in that genre was Arthur B. Reeve, who wrote a popular series of eighty-two "scientific detective" short stories featuring the exploits of Craig Kennedy, sometimes referred to as "the American Sherlock Holmes" (although, it must be admitted, Kennedy was a colorless character by comparison). Arthur Reeve also produced screenplays for Harry Houdini's mostly rather ill-fated forays into silent film and would later be commissioned by the notorious convicted murderer and millionaire, Harry K. Thaw, to write treatments for a series of films specifically on the theme of fraudulent spirit mediums. Their relationship, however, devolved into legal wrangling and the movies never entered production.

Into this heady milieu stepped Rose Mackenberg, who was ultimately to become perhaps the most enduring and prolific ghost buster of the 20th century.

Born in 1892, Mackenberg grew up in New York City. As a teenager, she developed a belief in spiritualism that lasted until she was introduced to Harry Houdini, probably during the late 1910s.

It seems that, when Rose first encountered Houdini, she had already been working as a private detective for some time. Their initial meeting may have come about as a result of her consulting with him regarding one of her own investigations, which involved a case of "spirit fraud".

Impressed by her faculties of logic, resourcefulness and quick wit, Houdini invited Rose to join the team of salaried undercover investigators that he was apt to refer to as "my own secret service". This clandestine team was primarily tasked with traveling ahead of Houdini's touring schedule, visiting towns and cities where he was due to appear and infiltrating the local spiritualist "scene" in disguise, to investigate and gather evidence of fraud. These details would then be passed on to Houdini, so that he could expose the fraudsters during his shows.

Inevitably, this tactic made Houdini many bitter enemies, angering both shut-eye believers who felt that he was attacking their religion and open-eye con-artists who knew that he was threatening their livelihood. Sometimes the hostilities between pro- and anti-spiritualists erupted into physical violence, and more than once Rose and other members of Houdini's "secret service" were caught up in the fray.

Partly as a safety precaution, Rose also became something of a mistress of disguise. Her first stop in a new town or city was to visit a department store and take detailed notes on the clothing worn by various local "types" of women, so she could plausibly pass muster as a Rustic Schoolteacher, a Small-town Matron or a Smartly-garbed Widow.

Her training with Houdini was clearly thorough, encompassing all the tricks of the fake séance trade and leaving her with eyes wide open, disabused of her teenage belief in the ability of mortals to communicate with the spirit world. Like her employer and mentor, Rose Mackenberg professed an agnostic stance towards the ultimate question of life after death, and had some sympathy for those shut-eye mediums who genuinely believed in their own powers and who practiced Spiritualism sincerely, devoid of conscious charlatanism. Also like Houdini, she was contemptuous towards open-eye "Spiritualists" who cynically took advantage of vulnerable people.

After Harry Houdini's untimely death in October of 1926, Rose Mackenberg vacillated about her future career and prospects. By that time she has become one of Houdini's most experienced investigators, with a wealth of experience in busting all manner of clairvoyants, trumpet-mediums, purveyors of love and luck potions and their ilk.

Mackenberg is known to have written a manuscript detailing her adventures in battling the "spook racket" - the final draft was titled "So You Want to Attend a Séance?" - but, sadly, it went unpublished during her lifetime and remains so as of this writing. The manuscript appeared as part of an eBay estate auction during November of 2012.

It's not unlikely, however, that her manuscript drew from the articles anthologized in this volume, which were originally published as a weekly series in several North American newspapers during the year 1929. It seems that, at that time, she had decided to retire from the ghost-busting business, perhaps intending her articles to serve as a final volley; in any case, her retirement didn't last long.

In a Movietone newsreel interview filmed a year or two before his death in 1930, Sir Arthur Conan Doyle - who was, clearly, still utterly sincere in his belief - stated that he expected Spiritualism to become recognized as "a great philosophy and, as I think, the basis of all religious improvement in the future of the human race." Two years later, Julien Proskauer - who was, like Houdini, a magician dedicated to exposing fraudulent mediums - estimated the number of people "suckered" by hoax séances, numerological and fortune telling sessions, etc. at 30,000,000 per year, and their losses at $125,000,000.

Rose Mackenberg persisted in her unusual vocation, investigating on behalf of insurance companies, law firms, Better Business Bureaus, newspapers and similar institutions. During mid-1945 she served as Chicago Tribune reporter E.W. Williamson's guide to the Spiritualist underworld of the Windy City; Williamson then revealed the mediums' predatory con-artistry through a series of exposé articles.

Rose also began performing lecture/demonstrations for service organizations, during which trumpets floated, tables tipped, glowing "spirit hands" materialized and Mackenberg generally did what she could to expose the tricks of the still-burgeoning spook racket.

She was, however, unsurprised when the US involvement in the Second World War engendered another revival of spiritualism - and then even less startled when it happened yet again during the Korean War. Interviewed in 1951, she estimated that there were then some 150,000 mediums active in the United States, and also noted that she expected that number to rise as long as the War continued.

By that time, Rose Mackenberg, known to her friends as "Mac" - a life-long "bachelor girl" who kept her New York City apartment well-lit because she had grown "tired of sitting in dark rooms" - had been investigating and debunking spiritualistic fraud for over three decades. Her "Spook Spy" exposés had been featured in the *American Magazine*, *Look*, *Collier's*, *Popular Science* and numerous other journals. Still, she noted resignedly that "no number of exposures, in fact, seem to shake the faith of believers."

Rose died at the respectable age of 76 years on April 10th, 1968.

Spiritualist churches still exist today, as do "New Age" trance channelers, professional telephone and Internet psychics and so-on. Despite frequent public exposés of prominent practitioners by print media journalists, television news investigators and professional detectives, as of 2013 the modern American "psychic services industry" was estimated to be worth slightly over two billion dollars.

Significantly, though, very few modern mediums attempt the sort of "physical manifestations" (ectoplasm, ghostly materializations, table-tipping, etc.) that were convincingly debunked as phantasmagoric tricks by generations of skeptics, prominently including Rose Mackenberg, during the first half of the 20th century.

Notes on this anthology

The language of the early and mid-20th century reflects some social attitudes towards race, gender, mental illness, physical disability and religion which have become deeply unfashionable today. We have faithfully retained the original authors' language as a matter of historical record; this does not, of course, represent an endorsement of those attitudes.

The original author's idiosyncracies of spelling, grammar and punctuation have been left largely intact, with only minor adjustments for clarity and context, to retain the flavor of the author's style.

Rose Mackenberg's articles were published as a series of weekly installments in several North American newspapers during 1929. The article ordering and certain textual details, illustrations, etc. changed slightly depending on the individual editor and publisher. This anthology represents a synthesis of those series, lightly edited to avoid repetition and redundancy.

The illustrations reproduced herein are the best available, given the scarcity of the originals and the variable quality of photographs and sketches printed on 1920s newsprint paper. Note also that, during the '20s, it was common for newspaper photographs to be lightly "re-touched" by hand for clarity, such as when the details of a human face, for example, would be sketched in if they were unclear in the original photograph.

Spiritualism, possibly true, and "spiritualism" demonstrably false

The three most fascinating and baffling speculations occupying the mind of this generation are the artificial creation of life by "laboratory birth", the possibility of communicating with other planets, and the fervent hope that our beloved dead may return and hold speech with us.

Of these three speculations, the last named has by far the most potent sway over our imaginations. In fact, next to the instinct of self–preservation, it is perhaps the strongest and noblest and most pitiable emotion of which the human heart is capable.

Mighty men of science have tried to convince people that spiritualism is an impossibility, that the grave ends all. But other men, equally great, engaged in similar research work, have held that genuine mediums, using genuine "controls," who seem to perform the function of a radio machine in transmission, can bring before the eyes of the believing the speaking phantoms of dead men and women.

Sir Oliver Lodge, renowned physicist and authority on the electron, has deeply rooted faith in the spirit world. So has Sir Arthur Conan Doyle, eminent author. So has the late William T. Stead, finest critic of his day.

Belief in the spirit world is, at root, a beautiful thing, but by trading on the sacred desires of the bereaved, fakers and charlatans have practiced frauds, eager to blind the gullible with the veil of deception.

To tear away this view has been the lofty and unselfish purpose of the truly altruistic, unwilling to see humanity bilked by a line and blend of its money by ghouls. Harry Houdini, master magician, spent a fortune and earned himself a vast enmity in an effort to wipe out spiritualistic chicanery.

And now today, on this page, the fearless and clever girl who was his secret, anonymous sleuth for years, and who knows perhaps more about this subject than any other woman living, begins a series of startling revelations about spiritualism – both spiritualism, the possibly true, and "spiritualism," the demonstrably false.

Rose Mackenberg, as a name, means, to the world at large, precisely nothing. That is what, during her work with Houdini, she desired. But now that he no longer lives she has retired, given up her amazing private detective work and has written a vividly compelling , obviously authentic account of the adventures through which she passed while ferreting out the secrets of mediums.

Begin it here – now!

Most self-styled mediums, with their spurious and specious methods, with their ghostly trumpets and spectral hands, hold few secrets – and fewer terrors – for me, as you will discover for yourself if you continue to read this series of articles.

After you have, for three years, invaded their séances in disguise, surreptitiously snapped flashlight photographs of the "wraiths" they have conjured up, joined and exposed their inner windings of some of their churches, as I have, the racket leaves you distinctly cynical – and not the least shade frightened, nor even surprised.

My secret service under the direction of Harry Houdini, the most superb worker of natural magic the world has ever known and one of the finest intellectual representatives of the human race, taught

Beatrice Houdini gazes at a bronze bust of her late husband.

me many things; self-control, courage, resourcefulness and the ability not to let myself be thrown off a scent by astonishment.

Staggering assurance

Yet even I have not entirely lost the ability to be surprised, I find. When I carefully picked up my morning paper the other day and glimpsed, on page 1, the headline, "Houdini sends from grave the word he promised wife," I was genuinely staggered.

I want to add, at this particular point, that my attitude, like that of my dead master, is neither spiteful nor biased. There may be such a thing possible as communication with the dead. I frankly don't know, and I want to be shown. It is an attitude I might describe as "mental agnosticism."

And I am convinced that there are a number of mediums who are not intent on looting their clients and who very devoutly and sincerely believe they are gifted with clairvoyant and clairaudient powers. It is not my intention to criticize them now, nor hereafter, and nothing that I shall write should be construed as reflecting on their characters.

Mysterious "tip"

But to get back to Houdini's alleged spirit message to his widow, Beatrice. The first intimation that Harry had actually "got through" a personal signal to Mrs. Houdini came on January 9, when the handsome widow, interviewed by a reporter who had been sent to see her on a mysterious "tip," admitted that the seemingly impossible, the thing for which spiritualists have striven for centuries to achieve, had occurred.

At her home, Mrs. Houdini, who for 30 years had appeared with her husband in vaudeville and other exhibitions, exclaimed, "Thank God!" She was visibly affected, but managed just to sum up the details of her experience. The message, she said, been sent to her in a secret code privately agreed upon by herself and Harry, and never divulged by either to a breathing soul. This code consisted of 10 words representing the first 10 letters of the alphabet, with combinations of the words representing the other 16.

The key was placed in a sealed envelope and locked in Mrs. Houdini's vault.

Mediumistic agent

The mediumistic agent who, reaching into the void, had been able to establish contact with the dead magician, said the widow, was Arthur A. Ford, editor of the magazine "Immortality," and head of the First Spiritualist Church.

As she told of the trance and the fruit which it bore, Mrs. Houdini was laboring from an excitement partly attributable to the psychic stress of hearing from the dead and partly to the fact that she was ill. She had fallen fainting in her home on New Year's Day, and as she had talked her dark, queenly head was swathed in bandages. Mrs. Balbina Rahner, Mrs. Houdini's mother who lives with her, entered in the conversation. Beatrice, delirious, had trilled out "Thank God, Harry, you're here!"

Mrs. Houdini had no recollection of crying out, but a few nights later she had dreamed that Harry appeared to her saying, "Thank God, Rosabelle (a nickname), at last you have found me."

On the following Saturday she had received a letter describing how Arthur Ford, utilizing a "control" named "Fletcher," sunk in a heavy trance and with his pulse beating lethargically, had received word that Houdini was calling.

Several witnesses

This letter was signed by Francis R. Fast, a broker: John W. Stafford, associate editor of the Scientific American: Mrs. Stafford and Mrs. Helen Morris, a zealous Spiritualist.

The translation of the ten-word code hinged on the phrase, "Rosabelle, believe."

Mrs. Houdini seemed utterly convinced of its genuineness.

The publication of the "great Houdini's return" naturally aroused a profound and earth-shaking sensation among the laity. If the story was provably true – and it was said that Beatrice Houdini and Ford were the merest acquaintances – it was the story of the century, an actual, factual miracle. For a flash even my composure was shaken. And then my memory began to function.

Not long after the Master's death, his biography, prepared by Harold Kellock, had been issued. I had, naturally, read it carefully, and my faculty of accurate reminiscence told me, dimly, that somewhere in that volume there was a reference to a code similar to the one that Houdini was supposed to have used in communicating with this earth.

A similar code

I hunted up the biography. Sure enough, on page 105, there it was. I give it here as a literary curiosity:

Pray - one

Answer - two

Say - three

Now - four

Tell - five

Please - six

Speak - seven

Quickly - eight

Look - nine

Be quick - ten

The Houdinis, said Mr. Kellock, had used this system of verbal signals in vaudeville as a "mind–reading" expedient.

Well, I kept my discovery to myself. After all, I had retired from the game. It was none of my business. And, besides, the affair began to assume the proportions of an amusing joke, which was sure to rebound on somebody.

Others were not so reticent as I. On January 10, a newspaper published, under flaring headlines, what it termed an exposé of the "big hoax."

The sensational message, it was affirmed, had been carefully rehearsed before it was sent to Beatrice Houdini. The gist of the exposé rested on the admitted fact that Ford was planning a lecture tour on spiritualism: the "voice from the grave" would, of course, have formed, and, to a point, did form, the basis for extraordinary publicity outside.

Doubt is cast

The newspaper sidelights on the non–authentic quality of the Houdini message had been preluded by loud utterances of marked suspicion from other quarters. Chief of the utterers was Joseph Dunninger, a psychic investigator of note, who regarded the whole affair as "the bunk." Dunninger it was who brought to Beatrice Houdini's sick room a man named Frank Pantino, a fish dealer.

Pantino claimed that Daisy White, who had been Harry's stage helper for several years, had been in possession of the code message. Miss White, who is an awfully nice, bright girl, was not unnaturally annoyed at this attempt to enmesh her in the controversy.

She dismissed Pantino's intimation that she had ever given Arthur Ford the code with the terse adjective, "nutty," and, while admitting that she had written many letters to Houdini, insisted that they had been purely professional, which I, for one, don't doubt in the least.

Meanwhile, the pro – and – con argument over the genuineness of the "voice from the grave" had become nationwide in scope. Many were found to uphold the integrity of the phenomenon. John W. Stafford, Scientific American editor, was staunch in upholding Mrs. Houdini.

"In this case," said he, "accepting the good faith of all parties concerned, because I know them all personally, there is no doubt that communication was established between a living person and a dead one."

In Boston, the famed Margery, one of the most publicized mediums in the world, with whom Houdini in life was on terms of "friendly enmity," manifested elation at the news of his supposed come–back.

Mrs. Laura Pruden, Cincinnati medium of much renown, created a diversion most surprising by announcing at this juncture that the message, as such, "didn't mean a thing."

So, when the hidden mechanics of the "voice–from–the–grave" were advanced theoretically, there was much mirthful rejoicing among the materialistic anti-spiritualists, and, I imagine, genuine surprise among those who had credited its authenticity.

Mystic cameras dupe grieved (with fascinating facts about ectoplasm)

Conclusive proofs

Of all the "conclusive proofs" triumphantly produced in their self-vindication by various Spiritualists, the one that might seem at first blush the most authoritative and undeniable is "spirit photography."

"You may not believe in materialization, ghostly trumpets, slate writing, or the like," a devotee of this form of "proof" may assure you. "But a photograph is a concrete thing, a roll of film or plate sensitized and exposed. What it 'catches' in the process is something actual, made visible, even if only for a moment, not something imagined; for the camera, having no imagination, cannot lie. If you doubt that there is life beyond the grave, just glance over these scores of photographs showing the living depicted in close conjunction with the dead."

I have given some years of intensive study to the question of "spirit photography," and I propose, in this chapter of my revelations, to show that such photography is almost invariably the result of (1) an error or blunder on the part of the photographer, or (2) a deliberate attempt to hoodwink the person to whom the picture is to be shown.

I do not declare flatly that there is no such thing as "spirit photography." I have sought earnestly and unremittingly and alertly for proof that it may exist.

I think it would constitute a touching proof to bereaved persons, longing for a glimpse of their dead loved ones, if a real spirit photograph could be found. But to date I have never come across such a photograph, made under fool-proof, water-tight conditions.

Always there has been the possibility of some leakage, some chicanery, or, as I say, of some odd blunder, innocently committed, which produces the effects of a "spirit photograph."

Of course, to anyone who has ever experimented with the camera, the average "spirit photograph" is a joke, and a bad one at that. The trick is so simple that it is a marvel the whole racket was not finally disposed of long ago.

Yet such is the great credulity of the human race, especially of that portion of it undergoing the sharp, lingering agony of personal loss, that this tragic traffic still find numberless dupes.

In the less-enlightened sections of the New World, as well as on the Continent and in the British Isles, it has flourished off and on since the sixties, and I see no chance of its dying out, especially with the marvelous new camera tricks and double-exposure effects invented by the German movie maker – all of which are calculated to be sensationally adaptable to the production of "spirit photos."

Details of "tricks"

I shall later on give the details of some of these tricks, with a brief account of how, even in the old days, it was possible to fake the pictures that have brought tears of recognition to gullible eyes and to responsive hearts.

Of course, these crudities will soon be supplanted by the new Teutonic method of photographing any given set of characters against any background, even though miles away. An astonishing invention – and how the mediums are going to eat it up!

As I write, two photographs, lying before me on my desk, tell the whole story of this form of deception better than any written word. One is a rectangular positive, showing on the left-hand side a close-up of a plump, young, rather sulky-looking girl. Her hair falls in dark masses un-bobbed over the forehead and down over the shoulders.

In the background behind her at her left is a luminous haze such as frequently obtains in the woodlands during lush summer autumn afternoons. Just beyond the rim of this haze is a pile of leaves on which is standing a supposed fairy of the most conventional picture-book type – a small figure in a low-cut dress, with long, pointed wings and holding what appears to be a bouquet of posies.

The fairy's hair is cropped, proving, I suppose, that it is a strictly modern fay, who wouldn't be out of date for anything. The fairy's form is remarkably flat in effect, almost as if it had been painted on the negative or transferred to it by decalcomania. The photographic quality of the small figure has nothing in common with that of the close-up.

Imposing on Sir Arthur

Yet this humorous, crude photo imposed on the credulity of no less renowned a person than Arthur Conan Doyle!

The picture of her sister was supposed to have been made by an English girl, a postmaster's daughter, in her rustic English garden. Sir Arthur gleefully accepted it at face value and copies of the print were forwarded to Canada, where its reception was much chillier, if a little more intelligently critical.

Certain spiritualistic believers thought it genuine, but when its mute evidence was laid before photographic experts, what they had to say was plenty – and very demolishing!

Arnold Genthe, one of the greatest of modern photographers, had some striking comments to offer on the fairy photo. While politely diplomatic in his attitude towards Sir Arthur's opinions, he thought the photograph either a freak of lighting or a childish, prankish joke.

Mr. Genthe affirmed that, with the use of small dolls and specially prepared plates, he could duplicate the little English girls' achievement — and shortly thereafter Harry Houdini himself made some "spirit photos"in his own laboratory that were infinitely more imposing than the importation.

But Doyle, as stubborn a fighter in his way as Houdini was in his, with bulldog tenacity and pathetic faith, refused to be shaken. He not only wouldn't admit that the fairy picture was an obvious trick photo, but actually republished his own monograph on "the little people," to which, on first publication, the public and remained hostile or indifferent.

He also printed new photographs of an alleged fairy, snapped at Thornton Heath, and German snapshots of a gnome and a "flower fairy" resembling a moth.

Touching credulity

His really touching credence and gentle simplicity of faith in the supernatural are naïvely expressed in the following words: "I have not seen the negatives or individuals, but I have collaborative evidence from people whom I can trust ... The characters of all the people concerned seem to have been excellent."

He found no persons of high intelligence to coincide with him. Dr. Walter Franklin Prince, then head of the American Society for Psychical Research and famous as the man who cracked down and laid low the Antigonish ghosts, regretfully gave us his opinion that the clarity of the original fairy photo was suspicious, and raised other objections as to its validity.

Houdini, a warm personal friend of Doyle's and a staunch admirer of his beautiful character and integrity, shrugged his shoulders and laughed softly when a print of the picture was handed to him.

"How was it tricked?" I asked him, for I hadn't then taken up the subject seriously.

"There are so many ways, Rose," he replied, "that I'll have to give you a regular lecture on them later."

He was as good as his word, and so I owe my knowledge of "spirit photography" to the dead genius.

Unintentional freaks

I have said that an unintentional freak of lighting has been responsible for producing extraordinary spiritualistic effects in photography. The other picture before me on my desk certainly proves that. It represents a "séance" engineered by that gifted and entirely honest magic worker and scientific investigator, Joseph Dunninger, in which he sought to prove, and did prove, that he could easily duplicate the mediumistic feats of a famous European psychic, Nino Pecoraro, who was aspiring to win $31,000 worth of awards for a convincing spiritualist demonstration, offered by "Science and Invention," Dunninger, Mrs. Houdini and Joseph F. Rinn. I will have more to say about Pecoraro later.

The photograph in question is a remarkably sharp and lucid snap. At the left are three men who attended the "séance." At the right is Mrs. Houdini, seated before a black table, intently gazing at the dark, glossy curtains masking the booth in which Dunninger is sealed, invisible in the picture.

A large square of white paper is fluttering through the aperture between the curtains. Not even the tips of Dunninger's fingers, holding the square of paper, are visible.

But this, while it certainly proves the adroit manipulative skill of Mr. Dunninger, is not the "feature" of the print. For at the top of the curtains, towards the left, appears what seems, at first, to be a gray blur.

Human face appears

Enlargement of the photo disclosed, much to the amusement and surprise of the skeptic who had staged the "sitting," the upper three-quarters of a man's face. The long nose, the high forehead, the deeply sunken eyes, the sharply cut line curving downward from the nasal flange – they are all quite perfectly realistic.

If any reader thinks, at this point, that I am "going spiritualistic" on him, let me banish all fear by giving the rational explanation of this "phenomenon." The gray, ghostly face of the "man" peering over the cabinet is nothing whatever but a thick wisp of smoke floating upward from the flashlight and reflected sharply against the black curtain.

These natural freaks of refraction are responsible for the many so-called "spirit photos" – they can prove nothing, except that the camera can, and often does, lie.

I have promised to tell you exactly how the camera can be made to lie, and I shall now try to do so clearly and without becoming too technical. I suppose the first hope of capturing a spirit on a photographic plate arose from the old superstition that, if a murderer bent over the face of his victim, a miniature reproduction of his face was imprinted on the victim's eyeball.

This is today an exploded theory. Yet as recently as 1908, the city coroner of Alton, Illinois, photographed the eyes of a slain woman and produced a negative that showed the features of an evil-looking, bearded man. How it happened, I don't know. It was probably a freak of the lens or some peculiarity in the retina or cornea of the dead woman.

A year later, along came Professor Hippolyte Baraduc, a French scientific investigator, who, in addition to snap-shooting such intangible things as "prayer, sorrow and anger," took a remarkable death–bed picture of a girl named Nadine, showing filmy emanations from her still figure and crisp electric flashes hovering over the bed.

The simplest method of getting "spirit photographs" is, of course, the ancient device of covering one half of the lens with cardboard or cloth, "shooting" the exposed half, then reversing the process with the cardboard and "shooting" the other half. Nor is the expedient of double-printing one to baffle the amateur photographer.

I, personally, have had some amusing experience in exposing such frauds. A friend sent me a photo from Kobe, Japan, of a man in the flesh, seated beside what looked like a woman in the translucent white draperies. The effect was good, but my friend was astonished when I pointed out that the "spirit" was lighted from the right; the living man from the left.

A "spirit photograph" with Abraham Lincoln's "ghost", staged by Houdini to demonstrate the technique of the double-exposure.

The misty image

There is still another way of getting misty illusions on a roll of film, which is to puncture the camera with a sharp needle, then arrange your "subject" and "shoot" him. If there is anyone standing within range of the needle–puncture you will find that person's misty image – it may be only an opaque blur vaguely resembling a human being – lurking on the negative when it is developed.

People like Sir Arthur Conan Doyle are too apt to forget that chemistry can play a vital part in creating "spirit photos." If, for example, you put a flask of uranium nitrate near a packet of plates, the strengths of the radiotrons will permeate the package and mark the plates.

The same is true if you put a coin and a pulverized gas mantle near a packet of plates; the strength shape of the coin will invariably be reproduced on the plate . The variations on this facile but effective trick are innumerable.

Ectoplasmic photography

I have referred only briefly in this chapter to ectoplasm photography, for one thing, because the practitioners of this sort of trickery are subtle and wily as contrasted with their crude brethren, and also because, while a great deal is known to biologists and pathologists about ectoplasm - a perfectly good scientific definition of the outer layer of a cell, the dictionaries are commendably call you about defining ectoplasy, a term meaning "to mould from without."

The word can be used in reference to any sort of materialization, but is generally employed by spiritualists to mean a cloudy, gauzy substance ejected from the mouth and then slowly withdrawn; a kind of ghost tissue that either represents the medium's visible contact with another world – like a psychic telegraph wire – or the actual presence of the person who has been summoned. The most skillful mediums have been, with luck, on occasion able to make this veil–like thing assume the vague proportions of the human figure, such as the celebrated Madame Bisson.

Actually the ectplastic substance that you see descending from the medium's mouth in most cases is one of two things – either the finely shredded or crumpled membrane of some animals lung (probably that of a sheep), or chiffon, so treated and doctored as to appear "spiritual."

Ectoplasm substance

The membrane or chiffon is wadded tightly into the cheek of the medium who, while she writhes in an apparently mystical seizure, is easily able to eject the stuff fold by fold. The ectoplasm spreads out as it emerges, and if it has been cleverly painted and shaped, may assume the aspect of a woman's or man's face.

Eva, the beautiful French medium, was able to make an ectoplastic substance take the shape of a large hand wrapped around her brow, but she was so long before my time that I can only guess at her method. Ectoplastic photographs have also been faked with thin strands of cotton batting, or thick cigarette smoke, but the most "advanced" of the ectoplasticists have recourse to an ingenious combination of concealed mirrors, indirect, dim lighting, and sensitized screens, which catch the reflection of a dummy concealed beneath the flooring and render it luminous.

Meanwhile the drawing at the head of this chapter will give you a capital idea of the impressions that are raised in the consultant's mind. Since most women visit spiritualists because of anguished bereavement, it is generally safe to assume that the applicant has lost her husband or lover. From the hidden trap the assistant manipulates the switchboard, and the figure of a man, with featureless face, appears behind the medium's head on the sensitized screen, while she writhes and groans in trance–like, galvanic twitchings, to the terror, astonishment and rapture of the young widow, so eager for a sight from "beyond."

Six $25 fees bought me six licenses to "marry and to bury"

One of Rose Mackenberg's ordination licenses, made out to her fictitious identity as Allicia Bunck ("All is a bunk").

"Crusade" and "crusader" are, to me, piebald words, half black, half white. Of course, you can use them to refer to the loftiest causes and the noblest people, but in ordinary conversation they are apt to suggest attempts at unjustified censorship, prying and snooping and infringements on liberty.

But when Harry Houdini and I swooped down on Washington, three years ago, to stamp out the menace of spurious "mediums," I must confess that my pulse beat a little faster; for I felt that our cause was just and that we had vital information to impart to the judiciary subcommittee which was conducting a drastic investigation into mediumistic activity.

Even before I got on the train, I had a premonition that they were going to be fireworks at the moment I started telling what I knew. I had underestimated my capacity to shock, frighten and enrage. It wasn't fireworks I touched off, but an emotional holocaust!

Those were super–strenuous days, filled with near–riots, a welter of conflicting testimony, shouted objections, muttered oaths, copious tears and the most marvelous, smashing demonstrations on the part of Houdini that a great part of alleged spiritualist power is fake and can be duplicated by any clever magician, who makes no supernatural pretensions, but is content to rest on his laurels as a performer and entertainer.

If your curiosity is aroused you can consult the documentary evidence of the period in the form of affidavits and direct testimony. There was a great mass of this, and the newspapers printed detailed articles about the probe.

Ignited emotional pinwheels

It was my testimony, brief and pointed, that touched off the rockets and pinwheels and giant crackers of startled emotion when wrathful persons broke in with protestations and shouts of "that's a lie!" and "we never did such a thing!" Ordinarily I dislike "scenes," but this pandemonium of unleashed hysteria was not only volcanically dramatic, but, to one on the inside looking out, extremely funny.

Washington has for years, you see, been thickly populated with mediums, and I must here repeat an important point that I made an early chapter of the series. I don't doubt for a second that there, as in many other cities, there are a number of genuinely devout, credulous people, who actually believe that they possess supernatural powers: that they can communicate with the dead and bring consolation to the perturbed soles of the bereaved. Of these amiable, well-meaning persons, I have no criticism to make, and nothing that I say should be construed as reflecting on their personal integrity.

When the chairman's gavel fell with a crash to signalize the opening of the inquiry, the committee room was packed to suffocation. Tense, anxious faces stared up into his, wondering what was going to happen. Houdini, calm, but with blazing eyes, sat quietly at one side, flanked by me, outwardly placid and inwardly intent.

Called to the stand, the master magician lost no time in launching as measured and savage an attack as it is ever been my fortune to hear. Distaining rhetoric and false courtesy, he tore like a whirlwind into the thick of his theme.

Doyle and Lodge "dupes"

"Honest and otherwise intelligent men fall prey to these schemers," he cried. "Sir Arthur Conan Doyle is the biggest dupe outside of Sir Oliver Lodge. Doyle has been misguided by "spiritualists" and has not seen the light. No one can forecast future events."

Houdini, unimpressed, but beneath his rigid self–command plainly irate, continued: "it is impossible to know what is going to happen to me or mine. And is it not strange that "mediums" have to charge a dollar or two for predictions when, every day, they could clean up a fortune by for telling what is going to happen on Wall Street?"

This pointed sally drew more hisses; also laughter from "disbelievers." Still Houdini's ammunition held out. "Lodge and Doyle," he remarked, returning to the two noted Englishmen, "are sincere, but deluded in their beliefs. Why, Conan Doyle even claims that I possess supernatural powers, when I can demonstrate that all the effects I achieve are by trickery and are nothing an ordinary man, equally skilled, couldn't do."

Then Houdini, who was a superb showman as well as a fearless and indefatigable seeker after truth, clinched his arguments by making the action suit the word. He revealed to the spectators, many of whom were frankly astonished, the actual methods by which some "mediums" produce "spirit voices." He delivered "spirit messages" to several of the committeeman.

Trumpet racket

In accomplishing this, he had recourse to the "trumpet racket," an ingenious device to which I shall devote some space in a later chapter. Several of the legislators, with the trumpet to their ears and listening attentively, declared that they heard the messages distinctly, although, on the face of it, neither Houdini nor any assistant of his was speaking into the instrument.

"You see?" Houdini said, with something like a small shout of triumph. "Just trickery." He was about to enter into the technique of the stunt when the committee suddenly adjourned, cutting him short in his exposé.

Up to this point spiritualism had not made a very brave showing in the investigation, but it did not lack its defenders, and quite warmly valiant ones, too. It was Mrs. Duncan U. Fletcher, wife of Senator Fletcher, who leapt forward with some fairly impressive testimony.

She had been, she said, an ardent investigator of spiritist phenomena for 35 years; had conducted successful séances in her own home, and possessed actual proof that prophecies made by mediums had been fulfilled to the letter. She had had messages from both her father and mother, and from "my own dear friends in the invisible world."

"They were not from George Washington, or Benjamin Franklin or Queen Elizabeth," she added with much sarcasm. "As to mediums giving tips on racing and stocks, it is not the desire of the spirit world to increase the pocketbook, but to enlarge the human soul."

Non-knowingly dishonest

Mrs. Fletcher's trump card, as she regarded it, was the fact that a violin lost by a boy years ago had been recovered as a result of mediumistic advice.

"I have known many ministers , doctors, officials and world-renowned writers who have had writings in the sunlight and in electric light without a cabinet or other paraphernalia, through a young girl in a deep trance . I have had dozens of such conversations and have had stenographic records of some of them … I have never come in contact with a medium who is knowingly dishonest. Some mediums have more power than others."

Houdini's expressed belief about mediums had, apparently, not only annoyed Mrs. Fletcher, it had also enraged the Reverend H. B. Strack, secretary of the National Spiritualist Association. Mr. Strack was dumbfounded that the committee should except the statements of a "confessed infidel."

Even Houdini was forced to smile broadly at this sweeping characterization, and you probably know as well as I that the reputed "infidel" was one of the most decent and God-fearing man who ever lived.

"My religion and belief in the Almighty has been assailed," he said in a graver voice. "I believe in God and will always do so. Come here a minute, Beatrice," the magician added, beckoning his wife to the stand.

Repudiating charge

Beatrice ("Rosabelle") came forward. Her husband took her hand and smiled into her eyes. "We have been married 32 years," he said. "She has starved – and starred – with me." He gazed intently at Beatrice. "Am I polluted or vile? Or am I good boy?" he asked her.

She beamed, a smile of complete confidence. It was one of the prettiest and most touching little domestic interludes I have ever seen, and should have convinced the most rabid antagonist that Houdini was on the level in all things.

But Strack was not to be put off the track with any such human implication of trust. He insisted that the committee differentiate in legislating between fraudulent and genuine mediums.

"The present law and license to a spiritualist," he said, "do not permit any medium to commit any fraud, any more than an automobile permit means that the driver can break any law. He has the courts. Those who have been robbed can have recourse to the police and the courts. I am just as interested as Houdini, and perhaps more so, and eliminating fraud in mediumship."

Mr. Strack claimed credit for cooperating with the police in several instances where mediums had come under suspicion and he "had it on them."

"We don't claim to be fortune-tellers," he exclaimed. Asked if spiritualists used charms, spells or philtres, he made a vigorous the Nile.

I want to emphasize at this point that these inquiring sessions were enlivened with a subtle and indefinable air of nervous mystification and bewilderment, with a feeling that, before the investigation was over, they would be revelations about spiritualism in high places involving mighty names, great reputations and the peaks of government officialdom.

Negative testimony

There were more than a few picturesque figures at the hearings. One of them was the veteran Remigius Weiss of Philadelphia, who told the committee that he had been investigating psychic phenomena for 50 years without having been able to convince himself that such things existed.

(Mr. Weiss, by the way, was one of the three persons to whom Houdini promised, if you could, to communicate with after his - Houdini's - death.)

Weiss went on, in great detail, to tell how he had unmasked certain "mediums of the past generation" and how he had secured sworn, written confessions from Dr. S___, famous in the nineties.

Representative Sol Bloom, author of the bill under discussion, displayed letters from officials of all the large cities in the country, in which methods employed in the various localities for curbing fortune-telling were outlined.

Washington, said the congressman, was the only city which did not have a statute forbidding the practice. Houdini pleaded against amending the bill to exclude spiritualists from the effect of its provisions.

The magician was next questioned by Chairman McLeod as to the individual beliefs of Arthur Conan Doyle and Sir Oliver Lodge, who, he said, he had heard were devout spiritualists.

Considerable surprise was expressed by certain committee members at conditions in the district as they had been set forth at the hearings. Most of the members seemed generally agreed that some legislation should be enacted to curb these conditions.

Freedom to spiritualists

The chief point at issue seems to be whether spiritualists ought or ought not to be excluded from the effects of the bill in order that their "constitutional right to worship as they pleased be preserved" – the phrase was Representative Rathbone's, of Iowa.

As the investigation progressed, interest in it grew intense. The newspapers entered the field, and an editorial in the Washington Times had this to say about Houdini's revelations:

"The historic old White House has been at the scene of many spirited social and private activities, but table tipping and spirit séances have never been recorded as among them. Spiritualism would obtain unusual prestige if it could be established that it had been given recognition in the home of the chief executive, even as a social diversion.

President Coolidge and his wife are little concerned, however, about spiritualism or other alleged mysteries with which Houdini, the magician, has been having such a hilarious time at committee hearings at the capital. The mental make-ups of the president and his wife are too substantial to lean in that direction …"

Houdini (front, left) demonstrates how a foot may be slipped from a shoe, even if the shoe is restrained by another sitter, and the agile toes used to ring a "spirit bell".

Scrutinize methods

I had preceded Houdini to Washington to pave his way with personal scrutiny of the methods of various spiritualists. Two especially drew my attention because of the elaborate claims put forward in their behalf by their admirers and followers. I shall refer to them for convenience and conciseness as Mrs. Q. and Miss Y. Each had a substantial and respectable clientele.

I consulted both of these ladies for readings, and with the results in my private book, sat back and waited development at the investigation. They were not slow in arriving. At one of the sessions soon afterward, Harry Houdini said, "Call Rose Mackenberg to the stand."

My testimony was as brief as it was consistent with my findings. I described my visit to Mrs. Q. And said that she had told me table-tipping séances were held "in the shadow of the White House," and that Miss Y. had told me that "almost all the senators" came to her for readings, and that she had specifically named four Senators.

Pandemonium follows exposures

I made it clear that during my brief stay scores of mediums and spiritualists had tried to get me to enroll in their churches, and that I had been ordained a "Minister of Spiritualism" six times, with, each time, a $25 fee. Authority to "marry and to bury" had been vested in me, I informed the investigators.

The effect of my simple statements was extraordinary. Pandemonium or panic would be too pallid a term to apply to what followed. With a clatter and a roar, local spiritualists who were present stormed up to the committee table, shouting incoherent defenses of their practices, and asserting in wild phrases their entire honesty and respectability. One man tried to attack Houdini, but was physically restrained.

"Houdini, though his methods may be drastic and sensational, is doing Washington a public service and exposing the ease by which fakers make money in this city. Spiritualism as a religion is one thing. Spiritualism practiced for gain is another. The followers of spiritualism as a faith are not responsible for reprehensible practices that have grown up here..."

Especially bitter in her self-defense was Mrs. Q. When reporters interviewed her later, she characterized my testimony as "a lie from beginning to end." At the hearing she appeared violently excited, as did Miss Y., to challenge my story from the floor of the chamber. The two women had risen from their seats waving aloft the money they had received, and demanding a hearing immediately. The committee vainly tried to restore order, but the hubbub was so great that that adjournment was the only possible move.

Magician's sincerity

In closing my account of the excited goings-on in the national capital as a result of Houdini's activities, I want to clear up one point with finality, I hope; the question of the magician's sincerity in instituting the investigation.

It was said of him, during the more hectic sessions, that it was "all a publicity stunt."

The people who impassionedly said these things were, of course, suffering from that mania for overstatement that always accompanies excessive nervous tension. It is true that Houdini was a most acute showman and never overlooked a chance for legitimate publicity. But he was also a fighting fanatic aligned against what he sincerely believed to be fraud and sham and greed, and if in that fight he, too, became excited, it was the excitement of profound belief in opposing what he pictured as the powers of evil.

Dwarf inside "psychic" drum causes exposé of Myra's mesmeric music

Ever since the ancient Egyptians learned how to make their statues "sing," the terrifying power of sound has been a valuable stock-in-trade of magicians and miracle-mongers. When to that power is added darkness, it is an exceedingly stout-nerved person who, under "Mystic" circumstances, can remain unmoved.

The fake "medium," on impressing clients to bleed them of ready cash, would find a singing statue impractical; he has, therefore, perfected and exploited sound for his cabinet séances in another way – he has devised a series of tricks with trumpets that have been, in the long run, hugely and unholily lucrative.

I want to take you with me, in this chapter, behind the curtains of an average cabinet hoax, and show you how really profound the effect of a musical instrument is, when it is apparently sounded by ghostly lips. And I want also to prove to you that such "manifestations" as this can readily be duplicated by any intelligent stage performer, with a little practice.

Myra's séance "too perfect"

The same affirmation holds true – at least, so far as my personal experiences go – with other forms of sound, including the beating of tambourines, the playing of violins, cornets and drums.

And, speaking of the last–named instrument, I want to tell you an amusing episode in which I participated during my work as a special investigator in attempting to ferret out "mediumistic" frauds. This was just prior to my association with Harry Houdini as his special detective, and it may have been that he engaged me on the strength of my reputation, slight though it was at the time, won by my exposure of this particular hoax.

Always interested in psychic investigation, though openly skeptical about most of the "phenomena" I have witnessed, I was one evening invited by a friend to attend a cabinet séance. She was not, by the way, an extremely gullible girl, and at her suggestion that the séance would be "good, clean fun," I agreed to accompany her.

Since the young "spiritualist" who put on the show – the clientele would have been horrified to hear it referred to in that way – was eventually exposed, reformed, and is now living happily as a married woman, I shall not divulge her identity, but merely refer to her as Myra. Gifted with remarkable beauty, intelligent, magnetic and clever, she had every natural factor to aid her in exploiting the "supernatural."

Myra was a cabinet worker; that is, she permitted herself to be bound, hand and foot, to a chair in a curtained recess. The draperies were then closed and the sound of cornets and other instruments could be plainly heard by the auditors outside. But Myra's trump card was a really adroit bit of inspiration.

As you doubtless know, most "mediums" never work with the curtains drawn back and the lights turned on – it would be obviously impossible.

No aid from darkness

But Myra, for the finish of her stunt, had an assistant pull back the curtains and turn on the lights. This time there was no sound of brass or reed instrument, but a very large bass drum that had stood on the stage throughout the "séance" began to give forth muffled, steady, rhythmic reverberations.

As a piece of clever psychological showmanship, the effect of this was very imposing; for the true believers in the audience, their appetites whetted for further marvels by the demonstration in the darkened room, never once thought that the bass–drum finish could be anything else but "immaterial."

I had my suspicions of Myra from the start. It was too perfect, too suave and well built up. I didn't confide my skepticism to my friend, who was plainly impressed, but a few nights later, effectively disguised as a respectable, bespectacled old maid, I gained admission to the circle again. This time I determined to do a little "materializing" on my own, and when the lights were first extinguished I "broke" the circle of hands – a simple trick – and crept around to the back of the cabinet.

Cautiously lifting the curtain, I stretched out my fingers tentatively in the direction of the bass drum and encountered – human flesh! His deformed little body compressed into an arc, a tiny dwarf was preparing to emerge. His nerve was marvelous, for he uttered no sound though he must have known that someone was wise to him. I decided to leave well enough alone for the time being, and returned to my seat in the circle.

Trickery Apparent

Myra's trickery now became apparent. Her "routine" was as follows: with the lowering of the lights and the drawing of the curtain, the midget – she "rented" him from a circus – would creep out – beat or blow the various musical instruments, then return to his hiding place. Then, for the grand finale, with lights up and Myra exposed to full view of the circle, he, screened from scrutiny, would add the artistic finishing touch by pounding like a fiend on the inside of the big drum.

Confesses fakes, retires

Myra did a flourishing business with this chicanery, though I warned everyone I knew that she was a skillful faker: but eventually her exposure came about and she withdrew from public life after a full confession of her misdeeds. We are good friends to this day, and I get an occasional letter from her.

Most trumpet "mediums" have not Myra's skill. The bulk of them – I do not refer to men and women who actually believe in "trumpet voices" – are clumsy frauds, and their clients are, for the most part, credulous and stupid.

Houdini (right) demonstrates how some trumpet mediums would "levitate" their props in the dark, by means of a false arm and hand.

But "the game" itself is interesting technically. I shall try to give a concise account of how it is worked, without entering boresomely into the mechanical subtleties that can be employed. These are virtually infinite.

D. D. Home, an incredibly facile and spectacular "medium," is accredited by students of psychic lore with having been the first man ever to exploit the trumpet effectively. This astonishing "medium" was a gifted musician, in addition to his spiritualistic prowess, and he was able to accomplish feats with the accordion which convinced his clients of his other-world communicative powers.

"Mystic" music hard going

Since the accordion is a cumbersome instrument to manipulate, it seemed to Home's followers nothing short of magic that, while bound, he could make the "spirits" perform upon it. But the secret of the performance was very simple – he had inside the cabinet a small, concealed air hose, which could be easily directed against the accordion's bellows.

Another expedient for producing "mystic" music is to conceal a small harmonica on your person (or, if you are willing to risk detection, a "giant mouth organ") and play it once you are shrouded in darkness. The remarkable similarity of the sound between a harmonica and an accordion can be appreciated only by a person who has tested both in the dark.

Harry Houdini, whose special investigator I was for three years, used to comment on the deceptiveness of the location of sound when no light is present. One of his favorite methods of demonstrating the fallacies of the human ear was to blindfold me and click two coins over my head, and then ask me from what direction the sound emanated. Invariably I thought it was in a corner of the room, or near the floor. Try this yourself, if you don't believe me.

I mentioned this acoustical freak because it helps to explain how many sincere people are deluded in cabinet séances with reference to the "geography" of noise. I have met and talked with scores of persons, of greater than average intelligence, who told me positively that they had heard the tambourines, trumpets and other musical instruments sailing over their heads. It doesn't call for the acuteness of a Sherlock Holmes to deduce that the instruments were entirely stationary and that lively imaginations, stimulated beyond proper judgment, had worked the "miracle."

Another way to produce effective sounds is by means of a bell under a glass cover, set in the center of the séance table, which is tapped in the darkness. Or you can use a duplicate bell, which is muffled. Then, by striking this, it gives the effect of the bell under glass being struck. Lacking a glass cover, one can put the bill in a paper bag or nail it in a wire cage – both expediences seemingly making it impossible to reach the concealed object.

Exposing trumpet racket

But it is, on the whole, the trumpet "racket" which most easily imposes itself on the credulity of "spiritualists" in town for the civic good. These gentry were "mopping up," and had impudently defied detection and coolly refused strong hints that had been given them to get out of the city before they were exposed.

The "dick" and the reporter disguised themselves quickly one evening and paid a visit to one of the better-known "mediums." They were received without suspicion – "mediums," although unusually crafty, can be amazingly stupid on occasions – and were admitted into the regular circle.

The "medium" rashly promised to materialize the "spirit" of the detective's mother, and, after the usual hocus–pocus of ghostly hands and fluttering veils, "materialized," with the aid of secret confederates, the form of the "old woman." Her high, squeaky, senile voice, startlingly like the real article, then began to intone broken phrases and to utter sobs.

Complete exposé

Although momentarily taken aback by the ingenuity of the deception, the sleuth had presence of mind enough, when the "ghost" approached him closely, to reach out and grab the supposedly incorporeal creature. "It," when the lights were turned up, proved to be the "medium," with trumpet in hand. The exposé was singularly complete, for, as the detective grasped the imposter by the wrist, the newspaperman flashed a light upon his startled face.

The investigators had planted a newspaper photographer on the premises, and an excellent reproduction of the "spirit's" face was obtained.

The most interesting feature of the exposé was the seizure and examination of the trumpet used. It was a long, cornucopia–shaped affair, capable, when pulled out, of an extension of three feet. When collapsed it was no longer than a man's hand. It was made of aluminum, which is an unusually light metal, and the joining of the rings, of which it was composed, had been so skillfully accomplished that even when they slid back and forth on one another the keenest ear could not detect the trace of a tinkle.

But not often can an investigator unmask fraudulence in so straightforwardly orthodox a fashion. Harry Houdini, sworn full of trumpet "mediums," was particularly adroit in trapping suspects, and I remember one occasion, in 1925, when he hits on an ingenious and successful device to snare the wily bird under suspicion. Like all good plotting, the scheme was simplicity itself, but I never heard of anyone trying it until Houdini put it to the test.

"Plant" on medium

This particular "medium" had been meeting with triumphs at every séance. His specialty was "spirit voices." Houdini, accompanied by a policeman and a reporter – all three in disguise – went to the séance (held in pitch darkness, as "light would hinder the control and perhaps kill the medium") in the guise of bereaved men anxious for communication with their beloved dead.

Following the usual songs and incantations, the awaited voices were heard. Houdini, who had disengaged himself from the circle of clasped hands, located one of the two trumpets used in the dark and smeared it with lampblack. Then at the height of the séance, when the "medium" had picked up this marked trumpet, the master necromancer shone an electric torch in his face and disclosed him to his astounded followers in the guise of a bewildered blackamoor.

This was one of Houdini's most thrilling disclosures, but an even more dramatic one was the unmasking of this is Mary Reichert, a Chicago medium with a tremendous clientele and herself a sharp–witted and agile woman. I reproduced the absolutely damning photograph of her that was snapped at a séance, but the case is so extraordinarily interesting that I should like to give some more details, particularly as I was one of Houdini's confederates during the exposé.

Mrs. Reichert, who lived on Emerald Avenue, invariably "put on the big show" in her basement there. On this particular occasion there were nineteen persons present, some of them believers, others Houdini's agents. I, working under an alias, had managed to ingratiate myself into the good graces of Mrs. Reichert and even after the speed flash had been pulled and the negative rushed out of the house, I stayed behind with another girl, Lillian Stewart, and consoled the sobbing medium for what "those terrible men" had done.

Followers Awed By "Chief Black Hawk"

Of the nineteen persons at the séance, eleven were believers. The rest were Houdini representatives, myself among them. At the moment that the flash was pulled by a daring staff photographer, Mrs. Reichert was doing her stuff with a vengeance. Employing a "telescope trumpet "such as I have already described, she was impersonating Chief Black Hawk ,"a dead and, therefore, good Indian," and her believers were obviously awed.

The trumpet, supposed to be floating around in the encircling darkness, was in reality held in the hand of the "medium," who, cautious of snoopers, had wrapped a handkerchief around it to prevent finger marks. Mrs. Reichert, I might add, had collected a dollar apiece from the consultants before the séance, for their share in the "revelations." So far as I know, she still has my dollar, but I don't mind in the least.

She had, by the way, pulled out the plug of the electric light so that – as she fancied – no one could surprise her while trumpeting. After the man had snapped the picture, in the basement where Mrs. Reichert invariably held her "meetings," the camera containing the priceless negative was rapidly passed from hand to hand of the operatives, and eventually reached the window.

"Tigress" Whallops Photographer

This window, opened on signal by an assistant of Houdini's from without, saved the day; for five of the magician's men, carrying and protecting the camera, climbed out. In the yard they were set upon by a relative of Mrs. Reichert, who had been, unfortunately, stationed outside the window as a lookout, on suspicion, as we learned later, that there might be some prying detectives at the séance.

"This woman," Houdini told me later, as he described with boyish humor the arduous endurances through which he had passed, "leapt at the photographer like a maddened tigress, socked him right and left, and clawed at his face, knocking his hat off. She still has the hat, a flashlight gun and a camera case," he added sardonically." And she's welcome to them. We knew what we wanted, and we got it."

An interesting sidelight on Mrs. Reichert's activities was the fact that, not content with one measly "control," she had recourse to three. One was supposed to be "Nina," a 10-year-old girl, who conveniently pre-empted Mrs. Reichert's vocal chords on occasions. The second was "Black Hawk," who was functioning so superbly at the time of the flashlight exposé, and the third was "Madeleine," a French woman, reserved, I presume, for consultants of a foreign extraction or birth.

These "controls" had a song repertory that ranged from "Yes, Sir; That's My Baby," to hymns. That otherwise intelligent people should fall for such a racket seems incredible; but you must remember that a mind wracked with grief, reaching out in the (literal) dark for any solace to a wounded heart, is apt to clutch at the slightest spiritual straw.

Blasé old London proves happy hunting ground for suave seeresses who thrive on credulity

Mediums who are convinced that they can evoke figures from spirit world and "mediums" seeking merely to grease their own palms abound in the Empire capital.

Belief in spiritualism knows no geographical boundaries. In China, oldest stronghold of extant civilization, the wraiths of ancestors receive paramount honor; Alaskan totems repeat the tale of the soul's return, and modern Canada has its devotees who woo the spooks with honest devotion and countless dollars.

But, I am convinced, London holds the palm for spiritualistic activities, genuine and otherwise. In that great, gray, blasé city, which has always prided itself on its imperturbability, drive hordes of mediums and "mediums" – the first-named convinced that they can invoke figures from beyond the grave; the others content to grease their own palms with the pounds and a shillings of the bereaved, made happy by a little ingenious hocus-pocus.

I have made a careful study of British spiritist records, and it is my intention, in this chapter, to give a brisk survey of what has gone on, and is going on, behind the cabinet walls and mediumistic veils of that proud capital, from the time that the grim–faced, soft–voiced Mrs. Fletcher was prosecuted in at the elegant eighties for alleged fake mediumship, to the present.

Let us first scrutinize the operations of the real spiritualists. There are many of these, and their intentions are noble and need no vindication. Personally, I have the greatest respect for such men as Sir Arthur Conan Doyle, Sir Oliver Lodge, the brilliant Horace Leaf, and William T. Stead.

I honor their aspirations, and it is with the most reverent respect that I point out that, in at least two cases, sharp mentalities have been colored by a sense of personal loss. This invariably makes for what the psychoanalysts term "wish-fulfillment," getting that in your dream life what your real life denies you. Both Sir Arthur and Sir Oliver lost sons during the war.

Douglas, eight, amazed London

The National Laboratory of Psychic Research, in London, has examined a number of odd and intriguing cases in the past five years. Certainly none of them has equaled in interest that of eight–year– old Douglas Drew. This astounding boy, of whose honesty I am convinced, has been for a year the topic on every tongue in England. Why? Because he is, so far as I know, the youngest possessor of a "poltergeist "on the record.

As good a description as any of a "poltergeist " is "a racketing spirit." Ever since the origin of the ghost story, persons have been recognized as being "possessed" by these curious manifestations. The classic case of Eliza Rose, in 1883, will occur to the reader. Eliza was a poor, harmless moron child who was adopted by a kindly Mrs. White.

The philanthropic matron could not have been blamed if she repented of her generosity towards the girl, however; for the very day she took the youngster into her home, weird things began to occur. Hot coals, unaided, bounced out of the kitchen; cream jugs rose and fell; hitherto silent clocks chimed the hours, and pitchers turned corners and smashed themselves.

It was not a very enlightened era, and we, today, can afford to smile slightly at poor Mrs. White's terror and her belief that Eliza's "poltergeist" was responsible for the rumpus.

The spiritists of the period worked themselves into a ferment trying to ferret out Eliza's secret, but they had just as little success as the British National Laboratory of Psychical Research has had, to date, with Douglas Drew.

A boy "possessed"

Their attention was called to him by his aunt, Miss Olga Ackerald, who, worried by the boys "possession by an unexplained spirit," wrote to Baron Blande, former secretary of the Swedish legation. The Baron, interested, took this child to the Laboratory, and then the cool-headed and rather hard-boiled examining board got the shock of its life.

They looked the calm and bright-eyed Douglas over; had doctors test his reflexes, which were nearly perfect, and got him to talk with a distinguished psychologist.

Then, with his affable consent, they put young Drew into a glass cage, stationed themselves around it, and awaited results.

What happened? They had given him some toys soldiers to play with. As Douglas, with evident relish, began arranging the little painted men in orderly ranks, others, not within his reach, fell over. He would turn around and right the fallen soldiers, but the minute his back was turned, the toys would collapse again.

The experiment was tried over and over – always with the same result. Conditions imposed seemed to make trickery on the part of the child impossible. Then how to explain it?

The conclusion reached was that Douglas was charged with excessive electricity, and that its radiations affected objects near him, but not within his reach. This sounds plausible, but sketchy. Why should such electricity effect objects not usually sensitive to it? How is the spark generated?

I should be interested to hear from readers who have theories about the Drew case, for during all my long period of psychic investigation with Houdini, I never came across a similar occurrence – a genuine one, that is.

In strong contrast to the Drew investigation, which though eerie, appears to be on the level, I want to tell you that the inside story of another case, in which clever trickery deluded a great many intelligent people and London was shaking like a leaf in a tempest.

It created the greatest post–war sensation since the signing of the armistice, and even to this day there are simple–minded, honest folk who will earnestly try to impress upon you the "fact" that "the cenotaph photograph was genuine."

It was this photograph which so stirred the minds and inflamed the imaginations of forlorn mothers and tragic fathers whose sons had fallen in Flanders Field. The picture's publication was the signal for an outbreak of hysteria almost incredible today – pathetic and unavoidable and understandable.

All London – with the exception of a few hard – headed individuals – thrilled to this "indisputable proof" that the souls of the departed are all around us.

As you probably know, the most solemn moment, yearly, of British life is the silence on November 11 when the populace pauses, with bowed and uncovered heads, and stands honoring those who died in the World War.

Annually, a mighty throng gathers around the beautiful cenotaph designed by the sculptor Lutyens, and refrains from even whispering. The silence is so terrific that it becomes almost as palpable a thing as actual noise.

Four years ago, two spiritualists of note decided that, if the public was ever to be convinced of the spirit photography, a snapshot of the crowds around the war memorial, possibly haunted by the ghosts of dead soldiers, might bring light to the unbelievers.

These two ladies were Miss Estelle Stead, daughter of W. T. Stead, the famous journalist, and a Miss Scatcherrd, both of the "Borderland Library," a spiritist headquarters.

I am convinced that these women were absolutely sincere in their convictions; that their sole object sanctioning the "ghost–gunning" expedition was to prove to the skeptical public the truth of what each devoutly and deeply believed about communication with the dead.

Before noon – when the silence occurs – Miss Stead and Miss Scatcherd made their way through the already thickening press of people and got as near the cenotaph as possible.

With them was a famous professional "medium" and her daughter. At the very moment that every tongue was stilled and every head bared, their cameras clicked. Then they departed to develop the plate – it was not roll film – and see what they had caught, if anything.

Under the ruby lamp a most astonishing spectacle grew upon the face of the plate, for not only was there a perfect reproduction of the Armistice Day throng – but, sweeping up in a soft cloud from right to left, what appeared to be a misty troop of soldiers, moving in a snowy arc that seemed to be propelled by a gentle wind.

Trembling with excitement, Miss Stead and Miss Scatcherd had positives printed and, with other spiritist friends, studied the picture intently. Both women had watched the medium steadily throughout the developing and printing processes and reported that they had been no chicanery on her part.

"Spiritualistic" curiosity

As a "spiritualistic" curiosity, I have reproduced on this page a copy of the photograph. It is really, in its own way, a minor work of art. The massed humanity around the cenotaph – the white bulk of the memorial itself – the sweep of the cloudy "spectres" – all contribute to a feeling of awe ... maybe.

The picture was widely circulated, and the bereaved men and women who had thought that life held little for them fell on their knees and wept for the sheer rapture of reassurance.

But others, more disinterested, whipped out their magnifying glasses and, with grim glee, set to work on the photograph. They made some very edifying discoveries. One was that, among these snowy "spirit" faces depicted were the visages of various celebrities who were known to be thoroughly alive!

One smart investigator actually identified the features of Battling Siki, the Senegalese prizefighter, who happened to be in America at the time.

Some of the boxer's spiritualistic admirers grew so alarmed over this that they frantically cabled him in the United States, pleading with him to "say it ain't so." Siki came right back with a highly humorous message; "Not even sick – Siki."

"Spirits" standing on heads

Another strange thing was noted about the photograph, that whereas all of the living people were turned towards the cenotaph, with their backs to the camera, all the "spirits" had a obligingly slewed around so that they faced Miss Stead and her friends.

And when it was pointed out that still other "spirits" were standing on their heads, even the most credulous smiled a little.

Ardent spiritualists rushed to the defense of their darling negative with arguments more vehement than final. Faces of the living presented as ghosts? Pshaw! These were the "astral bodies" of the living, invisible emanations from their bodies.

Why had the "spirits" turned toward the camera? Easy! They had sensed the presence of a "sensitive" in the person of the spiritualist and had directed their friendly gaze at her.

There was no explanation as to why a "spirit" should stand on its head.

The London Daily Sketch, taking the matter up, showed that its own expert photographers could produce equally impressive "spirit photos," given the same circumstances that obtained with Miss Stead's woman spiritualist, who, by the way, it turned out, had been permitted to take the package of plates home with her to "magnetize" them.

The seal on the package, Miss Stead explained, had remained unbroken. And besides Mme. Q___ was "incapable of trickery."

The Sketch editors offered a large sum to Mme. Q___ if she would produce another "spirit picture" under their conditions, which were quite lenient. But the "medium" flew into a huff, and announced that spirits were not interested in money. So that was that.

Miss Stead's final comment on the cenotaph picture was ambiguous, yet I consider her a thoroughly sincere, straight-forward person who would no more link herself to fraud then to murder.

Said she; "There is a great deal of subtlety in the subject that needs more careful study."

Poor girl! I can understand how anyone as deeply devoted to her dead father as she is can desperately hope for the truth of spiritualism.

Likewise, I can understand, if not applaud, Conan Doyle's stubborn resistance, in the naked face of the facts, to any denial of "spiritualist" rites, incantations and other pish–posh. The unfortunate novelist was bereft of his son by the war, and it is all too easy to see why he should join Miss Stead and other honest, but misguided intellectuals in their "search for the absolute."

Of Doyle's duping by the "fairy photographs" I have spoken before in this series (by the way, he was one of the first to rush forward and proclaim the cenotaph picture "absolutely authentic.") It might interest you, at this point, to hear, quoted first–hand, just what Doyle's conception of Fairyland is.

It is a place where quaint little figures, in green jerkins and crimson caps, ride through the "brake and the briar" on tiny horses – in short, the conventional Fairyland of a thousand more or less unimaginative writers.

Preposterous, you think? Perhaps, but no sillier than rich and gullible London society women who frequent the séance rooms of high–priced mediums a stone's throw from Mayfair.

You can see them there, late in the afternoon, little clusters of smartly gowned, bejeweled creatures with the inevitable stolid male escorts, chattering away for dear life and innocently unaware that their secrets of being overheard and jotted down by the unseen seeress, who, notebook in hand, is seated in an antechamber, listening to their talk through a slit in the wall concealed by an oil painting.

Common trickery

This is one of the commonest of tricks, but consultants of "mediums" seem never to have thought of it. So transparent, yet convenient a ruse, of course, puts the "medium" in possession of many important facts in the lives of their clients. Later, at the "sitting," she is able to divulge to her astounded audience things about themselves that "nobody could have known."

London has produced spiritist cases galore, some tragic, some farcical. Lying midway between the two categories was that of the late Lord Northcliffe's secretary, a Mrs. Louise Owen.

After Northcliffe's death, Miss Owen became involved in a legal squabble over the disposition of certain stocks left by the millionaire. The battle was to establish, by test, the validity of the sale of some newspaper shares, and when she took the stand to testify, she amazed her hearers by declaring that she had been in communication with Northcliffe's Spirit.

Automatic writing figured in the communication, Miss Owen claiming that, in the trance, she had received the following message from her dead employer; "This is too wonderful! I am full of emotion, exactly as in the old days." The action was dismissed.

Incredible graft in the sale of "magic charms, amulets and love philtres" is revealed

If you browse through old tomes on Medieval witchcraft, you will find amazing records of human credulity in the purchase of charms amulets, voodoo bags, lucky jewels and mystic oils. All very laughable, you will say, and childishly superstitious.

But if you venture into certain sections of London – or for that matter, into certain sections of any town on the continent of North America – you can find those same superstitious practices being freely indulged in and taken very seriously.

Today we are inclined to regard as utterly ridiculous the 15th century faith in the slaying of dragons to extract precious gems from the vitals; to sneer at the Black Stone of Mecca; to make fun of the belief that certain emeralds can cure the gout and goitres.

But I, myself, have, as Harry Houdini's assistant, penetrated to haunts and dives where, for "a certain price," I have procured charms "guaranteed" to perform the most miraculous feats, such as restoring a missing husband – I am unmarried – warding off bats and vampires and insuring me against the ravages of old age.

Truly, in the midst of so-called civilization, the miracle-monger thrives just as lucratively as he did in the Middle Ages. Scientific progress has been able to do little to cure our inherent gullibility.

Curative geegaws

The curative properties attributed to these geegaws by the mediums who sold them to me surpass anything that I have ever read in Elizabeth Villier's great treatise on the mascots, or any of the classic works on amulets, charms and spells, such as Montague Summer's "Geography of Witchcraft".

Yet these three small objects are, respectively, merely a flat rectangular stone, encased in a chamois skin; a twist of yellow cloth and a small cameo! I paid five dollars apiece for them. If you were to multiply that sum by the number of people in the world who believe in the efficacy of amulets, you would see what the staggering business the vendors of these charms can do.

Callous moderns were recently shocked and disgusted by the "hex murder" of a man named Rehmeyer at York, PA. Details of the crime, of which two youths and a boy of 14 with convicted, are too fresh in the public memory to need rehashing here, but the stir caused by the revelations about witchcraft incidental to the slaying shows how ignorant the average citizen is of the abuse to which the "powers of darkness" – so called – are put.

Monstrous superstition

To the clearheaded, it is nothing short of monstrous that people of primitive mentalities should actually believe that cutting a lock of hair from a man's head will banish a "hant," or that a victim of fever will immediately recover if a glowing coal is carried three times around his bed.

But the point I want to make is that, nine times out of ten, the people who resort to "hexing" and gratefully consult "pow-wow" doctors are family convinced of the efficacy of such methods I am no spiritualist, heaven knows, but I think the faith that simpleminded persons put in the alleged "black arts" can do irreparable harm in the community.

Even as I am writing these lines comes the news that the authorities have started a fresh secret drive against witch-doctors in New York City. I wish the officials luck, but I doubt that they will make much headway. The practitioners of the amuletic arts are firmly entrenched in the affections of their followers, and if a woman is fool enough to part with half the weekly salary for a phial of tinted water or a marked ball of yarn, who shall say that she hasn't a right to have her enjoyable folly?

Crafty charm sellers

I have personally investigated so many scores of cases that the mere recapitulation of them tersely would take up a page. Just to show you how crafty some of these gentry are in the way of "stage settings" and "effects" I will briefly describe a visit I paid to one vendor. It is typical of hundreds of other such investigations, only he "put on a better show."

Houdini had tipped me off that this man was doing a bustling business in a small town, and had dispatched me to get the low–down on the racket. I proceeded by train to the village – which shall remain nameless – and found that to locate the "witch" it would be necessary to hire a divver to a remote suburb and then proceed on foot to his house, which was situated in the rocky basin of a ravine.

Never shall I forget the weird spectacle that met my eyes. As I clambered slippingly down the rough and rocky path, the full moon rose and piercingly illuminated the patch of ground below. The house of the charm–and–philtre vendor was an unsightly cabin–like affair, in the doorway of which stood the bowed form of the aged "seer," beside that of his wife, who held aloft a lamp. The feeble rays from this flickered over the surrounding ground, revealing patches of white marble thickly scattered about.

The wily couple had established their "consulting room" in front of a graveyard! They had a genuine sense of "stage direction," of the effect produced upon impressionable minds by eerie, ghostly "props," and they didn't in the least mind living so near the reminder of this, so long as the customers continued to patronize them.

All hocus-pocus

Fortunately, I am not easily impressed by this sort of hocus pocus and I remained calm during the "consultation."

At the end of it I purchased two charms, assisted in the "blessing of handkerchiefs" and departed serenely for home. It was all most sublimely silly, but instructive in the foibles and fallacies of human nature. This man was later exposed and left his sensational-looking setting for parts unknown. I have no doubt he is today thriving under another name and doubtless working a different racket.

Inhabitants of large cities, however, need not preen themselves on the score that they are harder to fool than their rustic brothers. In the heart of Manhattan, "phrenology"– I do not refill to the genuine scientific attempt of that name – is a certain come–on for the gullible. Gypsies' palms are daily crossed with silver for transparent little "revelations," and nightly gaudily-robed astrologists promise everything from cures for warts to the recapture of an alienated sweetheart's love – if you have the money.

"Magic" powders

The favorite charms – the manufacture of which would scarcely bankrupt a proper – are neat rectangles of paper containing "magic" powder, usually simple coal dust, sifted, or pepper and salt. These charms sell for any sum, ranging from a quarter, in the slums, to two dollars and a half in the better sections.

For getting a "spell" on an enemy – as in the case of the hex slaying – the fee is, of course, perceptibly higher, but if anyone with the "evil eye" is bothering you surcease can be had, or at least promised you, for the price of three packets of cigarettes.

The nomenclature applied by these soothsayers is quaint in the extreme, and indicative of the sources – many of them Medieval – of modern "black art." Half a block from Broadway you can buy samples of the Devil's Shoestring, Adam and Eve Root, John the Conqueror Root, French Love Drops – to ensure the return of a faithful suitor – Lucky Black Cat Wishing Bone, Spanish Drawing

Lodestone Powder, Attractive and Quick Luck Oils and Anointing Oil and Mystic Dust.

Impudent coolness

"Healer" salesman of these charms face serious opposition, every day of their lives, from the police, the public prosecutors, the city health department, the Attorney General, the medical societies, the spiritualist baiters, like Houdini, as well as former dupes who have revolted against such practices . Yet their impudent coolness remains unshaken.

One reason, of course, why this is so, is that the making and vending of charms is, comparatively, a cheap and easy matter. Where a regular "consulting medium," in order to mop up the dollars, has to establish herself in a residence with a séance room and other cumbersome and costly trappings, and leave herself open to raids, the amulet and philtre "experts" can conceal their wares in their pockets, and, too, can do business in a jiffy on a street corner, in the subway, or even in bright daylight

A survey of any city's "charm belt" would show – and I can prove this by quoting from my personal notebooks – that its range extends from the lowest sections to the highest. All are prolific sources of such manifestations. Superstitious Negroes offer the quickest "turn–over," but there are countless "spiritualists" and "witch doctors" who disdain any clientele except what is known in the theatrical problems as "carriage– trade"; this is people wealthy enough to afford automobiles.

Wiley and furtive

In the fashionable, aristocratic and exclusive sections, the more fashionable brand of charm–dispenser and soothsayer can sometimes be unearthed – but not often. He is a wily and furtive creature and the cruder methods of come-on razzle–dazzle find no favor with him in his dealings.

His usual procedure is to rent a comfortable but not ostentatious little apartment, taking good care that the address is a "nice" one. This he outfits with painstaking taste. He never runs the dangerous risk of advertising, trusting, instead, to an invaluable, human tendency to do his advertising for him by word-of-mouth.

This negative policy usually bears juicy financial fruit: for it is a common desire to seek out and consult "esoteric" people who seem to be denying themselves to the general public.

This type of "mystic" you will generally find coy in making appointments, so that your appetite for his mysteries is automatically whetted. I have personally investigated eight of these cases, but only in one instance was I able to get the goods on the soothsayer.

They are wary birds and to fight them takes both time and money. For besides their shrewdness they are generally in possession of ample funds, due to the exorbitance of their charges and the fact that most of their patrons are men and women of independent means.

A grotesque, but fully documented, instance of the gullibility of the rich and influential came to light recently when it was disclosed that two United States Supreme Court judges, an enormously wealthy widow and a learned professor of Greek had been clients of one of these "hideaway mediums."

This particular specimen announced himself not only as a "mystic," but also as a "healer." He could have "cured" any form of malady, he told me, including "peevishness" and the smoking of tobacco. His treatment may have eliminated the first–named "disease" from my system, but I am afraid I still like my cigarette.

Cannot believe anything

The "professor" did not rely entirely upon his otherworldly powers, his amulets and philtres. He had also invented a most pleasing little machine composed simply of two electrodes. By grasping these firmly, the patient was cured of any malady - mental, physical or spiritual - after 15 minutes. Truly blessed are the feeble in brain, for they can believe anything!

But it is, perhaps, in certain parts of Brooklyn where the charm mania runs most happily rampant. A cozy coterie all of "spiritualists," recently disbanded of their own accord – things were getting a little too hot for them – did a land office business in charms. Strung beads and brightly colored bags containing ground-up roots were among their most valued offerings to distressed humans.

I went to one of the séances – the most amusing experience – and was surprised to find that attendance at the sitting cost only two dollars. The ante was swiftly raised, however, to five when an especially "difficult case" demanded praying over the consultant.

I was reminded, by some of their incantations, of the historical "Stones of Healing" that were employed in the olden days by people who believed, or who said they believed, that the touch of a ruby or coral would "remove discord" between husbands and wives.

There was scarcely, then, a single precious or semi–precious stone, from the diamond to the sydonyx, that was not believed to have magical curative powers. The modern practitioners of the "black arts" have carefully nurtured this superstition and kept it alive, although my little playmates were content to use jade and even colored pebbles.

High–priced specialist

I knew – but "not socially"– one voodooist who could be accounted a really classy vendor of charms. His prices were high – $1000 for a Black Cat's Wishbone: a bottle of cat's ankle dust, $50: New Moon powder, $25, and King Solomon's Marrow, $1500. He also specialized in the common forms of cure for "hants," such as Guffer Dust, rabbit's feet, silver-plated bullets – he had evidently read "The Emperor Jones"– carved elephants and incisor teeth from dog's jaws.

So pretentious did this individual grow – I believe his income was estimated at $7000 a year – that eventually he came to regard himself as a real power in 20th century society, and he bull–dozed and bamboozled his clients with such effrontery that, eventually, he dug his own financial grave. Some of them complained to the police, and a speedy conviction followed, to the astonishment of the crestfallen "mystic."

Not all of the voodooists are black and some of them are sincere but they have to be cautious and many of them list themselves as "Doctor So – and – So." They are too foxy to fall into the trap of calling themselves M.D.s, which would bring them into the dreaded limelight of the law.

My next chapter I shall devote to Harry Houdini, the greatest master of natural magic who ever lived as a personality, with little personal touches of characterization that only one who had worked with him for years could provide. I shall tell about his disguises and escapes – and finally I shall tell you about the only spiritualist phenomenon for which Houdini could never find an adequate explanation.

Many spiritualists claimed Houdini had power to enter Fourth Plain, dissolving material body

I want to devote this entire chapter to honoring the memory of a great man. My recollections of Harry Houdini, champion magician of the world, are so vivid that they are etched on my brain as if by acid.

I remember not only the spectacular psychic investigations he and I conducted, but little intimate things about Houdini himself – small oddities of temperament , tricks and forms of speech and gesture, his humanness, his lovability, his sudden, tempestuous bursts of anger, his worshipful love of his wife, his shyness, his magnificent sense of the theater.

Wanted to believe in spirits

You will admit, I think, that in this series of articles I have told you many surprising things. But at this point I am going to tell you something that surpasses even the most incredible of my former revelations.

Harry Houdini, from the bottom of his fine soul, wanted passionately to believe in spiritualism!

You think I am romancing, indulging in fantasies? Not at all; Houdini, who all his life had filled at him the epithets, "ghost-baiter," "spook-chaser," "foe of the psychic life," would have sacrificed a fortune if he had ever been able to convince himself that there was actually such a thing as communication with the dead. I think he would willingly, gladly, have thrust his right arm into fire to receive a genuine message from the spirits.

And his relentless and almost religiously fervid attempts to ferret out and unmask fraudulent "mediums" were devoid of malice. He sought but one thing: truth.

You may ask why the master necromancer was so desirous of establishing the provable truth of spiritualism. One word will answer the question: mother. Houdini's mother was, to him, the most wonderful woman that had ever lived. She represented an ideal to him, precious, pure and adorable, and when she died he was inconsolable.

Harry Kellock, in his excellent biography of Houdini, published by Harcourt, Brace and Company, writes:

"Quite aside from his professional genius, he was a rabbinical puritan, with much sentimentalism in his make-up and a streak of mysticism.

While he devoted his life largely to devising methods for the breaking of physical bonds, he was also interested in breaking psychic bonds and communicating with friends who had passed through a door for which he had no pick-lock. After the death of his mother, his curiosity developed into a passion."

Tenderness inherited from mother

I have before me, as I write, a rare photograph of the old lady. It is worth studying for two reasons; the deep, charming, infectious humanity of the smiling face, and the firm mouth and aggressive chin, heritages handed down to her son. She must have had, I think, those are balanced qualities of poised power and innate tenderness which were his, too.

Other photographs in my position include snapshots of the handcuff king, with his mother, walking along the street.

These pictures are remarkable in that they tell of Houdini's reverential devotion to the "greatest woman in the world." In one picture he is gazing at her with an intense ardor in which psychoanalysts would doubtless detect traces of "mother fixation."

She returns his gaze with a look of mellow gentleness.

In the other, he is kissing her goodbye, having deposited is pathetic little black traveling bag on the sidewalk for the purpose.

What a far cry from those early days of Houdini's struggle against public indifference and comparative poverty to the later, glittering, glamorous time of his universal fame and acclaim.

Yet in all those years his attitude towards Mrs. Cecelia Weiss, whose fifth child he was, never flickered a hairsbreadth. Dying, he left behind for Beatrice, his wife, a secret note, saying that in all his life he had loved only two women – her and his mother.

I have said that Houdini, hard-boiled as his attitude was towards what he regarded as "spiritualistic" trickery, was constantly tormented, and tried to establish the demonstrable truth of spiritualism as a doctrine. Let me illustrate that remark by giving you an account of a "spirit message" he received during a visit with Lord and Lady Doyle.

Skeptic despite Lady Doyle

Lady Doyle, wife of Sir Arthur Conan Doyle, proposed a special séance for the master magician, who was for years a warm friend of both, and Houdini accepted the invitation willingly. Hoping that conditions would prove more responsive if no other "personal force" were present, the Doyles politely requested Mrs. Houdini not to attend the séance, and she acquiesced with her customary tact.

Houdini and Beatrice had a secret code that they had used in vaudeville, whereby , through the most innocent-appearing gestures, they were able to communicate silently with one another.

Just before Houdini left with Sir Arthur, Beatrice wigwagged her husband in an unostentatious pantomime that the previous night she had told Lady Doyle at great deal about his early life, with a special stress laid on his relations with his mother. She had even confided to Lady Doyle such intimate little details as the fact that Houdini, while with his mother, never wore any clothes except those she had given him, and had described his habit of impulsively laying his head against her breast so that he could hear the rhythmic beating of her heart.

In the Doyle's suites, Sir Arthur drew the blinds to exclude the bright light, and the trio sat down at a table on which there were pencils and pads. All three pairs of hands were placed precisely on the surface of the table. Houdini's attitude, as he related it to me later, was certainly one of saintly tolerance and decency.

"I resolved," he said, "that I would be as religiously minded as was possibly consistent with sincerity, and not once did I scoff at the ceremony. I not only was willing to believe, I was eager to believe. My heart beat violently at the thought that at last I might be able to penetrate the veil and stand in the presence of my adorable mother again. To see her, to hear her, would have meant the purging of all pain that hung heavy about my heart. I tried to put away all the doubts that had assailed my brain for thirty years."

It was the birthday of Houdini's mother.

Ensuing manifestations were weirdly dramatic. Lady Doyle was observed by the two men to be in the throes of some sort of tremulous seizure. The hands palpitated and beat the table; the voice shrilled; she called feverishly to the spirits to "send me a message!"

Sir Arthur tried to quiet her, but, impelled by some invisible force, she snatched a pencil and began to write "automatically."

"Spirit" dictation

Hoping desperately that at any moment his mother's presence might become apparent to him, Houdini sat serene and observant. Meanwhile, the fingers of Lady Doyle's right hand, propelled as if by some furious, dominant wind, drove mechanically across the paper. The letter that her "spirit" dictated is far too long to quote extensively, but a paragraph will give its flavor of hysteria:

"Oh, my darling, thank God, thank God, at last I'm 'through' – I've tried, oh, so often, now I am happy. Why, of course, I want to talk to my boy, my own beloved boy. Friends, thank you with all my heart for this. You have answered the cry of my heart."

Houdini told me later that at no time did he have the faintest perception of a genuine contact with the beyond. He was shaking, yes, just as any human being would be at the mere notion, no matter how improbable the pure reason would assert, of being contacted with a blood relative, but his mind was far too firm to be veiled with emotional irrationality.

An example of the famous clear-headedness came out in his statement that his mother had never learned to speak, read nor write English, despite her fifty years of residence in the States. The claim made by spiritualists that "spirits became better educated in the realms beyond" left him quite cold.

But, let there be no doubt about it, he was all along firmly convinced that Sir Arthur and Lady Doyle were a million miles removed from personal trickery. Houdini believed that when Lady Doyle became the medium of "automatic writing," she actually she thought that she was "possessed."

He never for a second challenged the purity of their intentions or creed – he merely thought that many of Sir Arthur's published statements were hysterical and wide of the mark.

Spasms of annoyance

One of the things in his career that threw Houdini into spasms of annoyance was the bull-dog tendency with which various spiritualists and, indeed, international celebrities insisted on claiming him as their own.

Doyle always insisted that Houdini's extraction of himself from straitjackets, torture cells, jails and other confinements was the result of "dematerialization." Despite Houdini's comically vehement denials, Doyle maintained that faith without break, and another English spiritist/investigator, who watched Houdini's more subtle and almost undetectable tricks of disappearance and reappearance, wrote to the press that Houdini was able to enter the Fourth Plain (i.e., dissolves himself bodily.)

Houdini's boyish petulance with such nonsense was one of the most amusing of his many mercurial moods.

But there were times when his genius for natural magic had results that couldn't have been foreseen , when his sensitive, gentle heart was wrung by the sudden knowledge that he had quite unwittingly implanted "belief "in a susceptible person.

Houdini and Bernhardt

I remember the meeting between Houdini and the late Madame Bernhardt, "Golden Sarah." The great actress , who was by no means a visionary, gullible fool, had witnessed certain of the Houdini tricks at a private performance especially staged for her. Visibly impressed and puzzled, she sat beside Houdini in the taxicab as they rode slowly down Broadway.

The divine Sarah – beyond any doubt the most sublime actress of her era, looked secretively at the magician , then her glance stole down towards the hem of her dress. She must've been thinking of that cruel, necessary operation that had deprived her of a leg – an unspeakable, unthinkable tragedy to a woman whose art depended partly on the graceful posture of her body.

With a hint of a tear in her golden voice, she finally said softly; "Dear Mr. Houdini, will you do me a great ... the greatest favor? "

Houdini, astonished, replied: "But certainly, Madame. Anything that lies in my power."

"Then" – and the golden voice sank softly, deprecatingly, as if the owner were overcome with her own demandfulness – "then, won't you please restore my leg?"

Houdini was horrified, touched and at a loss for adequate, consoling words. But he finally called up enough courage to tell Madame Bernhardt gently that his powers, such as they were, were only mortal, that they had no supernatural might. The actress silently shook her head. She had seen him work "miracles"; why couldn't he - wouldn't he work this healing wonder for her?

Truly, a touching, a devastating experience for the deeply emotional Houdini.

Could make it rain – and stop

But the necromancer's other experiences were not always tear-compelling. Some of them, as unfolded by him with that odd mixture of sly naïveté and sound psychological sense, were extremely funny – certainly none the funnier than his "astounding performance" – on the surface, it certainly was that – at the home of his friend B. M. I. Ernst, at Sea Cliff, Long Island.

Mr. Ernst, Houdini's close friend and legal advisor, had asked the knot-defier to come down and entertain some friends of his son, Richard. What happened there, Houdini used to refer to laughingly as "my greatest feet of deceit."

Mr. Ernst had prepared an elaborate fireworks display for his young guests, but nature, perversely, defied the pyrotechnics. A furious rain and wind storm broke loose; the rockets and Roman candles were beginning to be drenched, and the children were on the point of tears. Richard, the dismayed honor guest, rushed up to Houdini, trembling with anxiety, and cried:

"Mr. Houdini, Mr. Houdini! They say you can do things no one else can. Please make the rain stop."

Without a second's hesitation Houdini petted the boy on the head, with the reassurance: "Why, Richard, of course I can."

Raising his hands in a theatrical gesture, he thundered towards the heavens:

"Rain and storm, I command you to stop!"

The first mandate proved ineffective, so Houdini repeated it three times. As if by magic, the skies cleared, the sun came out, and the happy children resumed their interest in the fireworks.

But Richard, we found out, was a naturally clever skeptic, and when the show was over, he sidled up to Houdini with a wily gleam in his eyes, and said quietly:

"Hey, you know it would have quit raining anyway!"

For most magicians this would have been a fatal poser, but Houdini was game. Glaring sternly at Richard, Houdini again raised his hands and shouted:

"Great Commander of the Rain, once more let the water flow to earth and allow the flowers and trees to bloom." Instantly – to Houdini's secret surprise – another violent downpour started.

"Make it stop ! Make it stop again!" The delighted children screamed.

But Houdini had gambled on probabilities twice and won. He wasn't taking any more chances.

Houdini was fond of children and animals, too, although he employed comparatively few in his acts.

Made elephants "disappear"

But, now and then, Houdini, as if to "keep his hand in," would devise and perfect some illusion with an animal that left his public astounded and even his closest friends gasping. I remember vividly his "largest" experiment in point of poundage.

It was performed with a gigantic elephant, weighing, according to the official standard scales, just a shade over five tons.

For the elephant trick, Houdini practiced incessantly.

His first move was to win the beast's friendship and trust. This wasn't difficult. Next began the nerve-tearing, tedious routine of rehearsal. I recall one of these "séances," as he called them, with his invariable small-boy humorousness.

When the monstrous quadruped reared on its hind legs, with the small figure of Houdini beneath the padded paws, and began to sway, two of Houdini's girl assistance became terrified lest he be crushed. They rushed forward, shouting warnings, but the imperturbable Houdini waved them away. His only emotion was one of annoyance that hysteria had broken up his rehearsal.

As performed on the immense stage of the hippodrome, the act "panicked them." It opened with a clever routine, during which Houdini, while apparently tantalizing the beast, was in reality pacifying and cajoling him.

After Houdini had apparently hypnotized Jumbo, the latter ponderously stepped into a cabinet just large enough to shelter him and the curtains were drawn for a matter of some forty seconds. When they were flung back – no elephant!

The trick, which, by the way, was cited by some ardent spiritualists as another evidence of Houdini's ability to dematerialize people and animals, has never been solved. Trapdoor escape for the cabineted beast was impossible because beneath the stage flooring were the waters of the huge hippodrome tank.

Houdini's death

Houdini's death, sharply and tragically unexpected, must fittingly occupy the last paragraphs of this chronicle. It would be interesting, if not important, to record a belief in Sir Arthur Conan Doyle's intimation that this came about as a result of a medium's prophecy and that, at the end, the stricken magician conversed with the spirit of Colonel Robert Ingersoll.

These are the purest fantasies. What really happened was that Houdini, his ankle broken during the performance of the Chinese Water Torture Cell trick, was lying down in his dressing room at a Montréal theater before a performance, reading his mail.

Two students at McGill University came in to chat with him and were followed by a third. The latter asked Houdini how heavy a blow he could sustain with impunity. Houdini, absentmindedly continuing with his letters, replied that, if warned, he could absorb almost any sort of blow.

The youth impulsively hit him four times on the abdomen – and that was the beginning of the end. Though he continued to perform with epic fortitude on tour, it was found that his appendix was gangrenous, and the operation for peritonitis was a foredoomed failure because the disease was so far advanced.

Houdini's coffin arrives in New York City.

Millionaire "medium" rejects Houdini's $10,000 challenge that he'll duplicate "feats" by magic

Houdini (right) demonstrates how, having loosed rope restraints, a fraudulent medium can use an extendable wand to write on a chalk board.

John Slater Proves Most Mettlesome Foe to Man of Fake-Exposure

Houdini's activities lead to a wild riot

John Slater, millionaire medium, was one of the most mettlesome foes who ever engaged Harry Houdini's mental rapier. Gifted with charm and skill, and worshiped by spiritists the country over, Slater ardently disclaimed great wealth.

In his determination to "turn up" Slater, Houdini unwittingly paved the path for a series of rumpusses and riots that stretched from Philadelphia to Chicago. Heads were bludgeoned and blood spilled in those exuberant days and I count myself lucky to have escaped the fracases with a mere bruised ankle and some pungent memories of the general roughhouse, which I shall try to set forth accurately.

By chance I was not mixed up in the Philadelphia imbroglio, but the Chicago mix-up took place before my very eyes.

I want to go on record right now by saying that I have no charge of fraudulence to press against Slater. I am willing to believe that he believes in his own capacities and, for all I know, his powers may be real. The fact that he is well-to-do would seem to be an argument in his favor, for you will seldom hear of phony mediums possessing wealth.

Both Slater's avowed enemies and warmest friends concurred in calling him "the cleverest message-reader in the world" – only, of course, the spiritualist meant by "clever," "inspired," and the agnostics, "adroit." There was something very engaging in the man's personality, and although I never had the faintest faith in his supernatural powers, I could see how he had endeared himself to thousands.

"Personal magnetism" is really more of a miracle then trumpet speaking, slate-writing and ectoplasm.

Hand-picked aides

Houdini's personal staff of investigators numbered twenty men and women – mostly girls like myself, for mediums aren't apt to suspect them - but for this particular assignment there were selected only five, all "hand-picked." We worked, independently and together, on as rigorous a schedule as a train dispatcher or a stagehand. And our routine proved surprisingly productive.

You may wonder, at this point, just why Harry Houdini bothered with assistants; why, with his marvelous brain, he didn't visit the mediums himself, and assure himself, at first hand, of their fraudulence or their honest intentions.

There are two answers to that question. One is that no man in the world, for all his brilliance and energy, could possibly "cover" the whole territory that the master magician had mapped out; secondly, although he occasionally visited mediums in adroit disguise, Houdini's features had become so widely known as those of a "spook-baiter" that he would have been recognized nine times out of ten.

As a matter of fact, one of the boys with whom I worked was himself recognized; but I am getting ahead of my story.

Houdini, before our departure for the middle west, had given my four colleagues and myself the most meticulous instructions as to how we would work the "racket." As this schedule formed the basis for almost all the subsequent psychic investigations I made, working by myself, I will give the details of the plan.

The five of us registered - at different hotels – under assumed names. One of my favorite noms-de-spook was Ruth Masch, although I have employed as many as seven at different times. Next we would proceed to visit various neighborhoods, rapidly spot the addresses we wanted, then arrange for a consultation with the medium.

Prearranged stories

Of course, we all had prearranged stories about having lost husbands or wives through death or desertion, or else we wanted to get in touch with the spirits of our dead children. Some of the yarns were spun with the most outrageous fabrications: in fact, the more fantastically improbable the story, the more apt was the medium to fall for it.

Memorization of the medium's features was an important part of the job, so that when we reported back to Houdini we might be able to give him a workable mental photograph of the person he intended to expose. His ability to identify mediums in his thronged audiences was invariably dramatic, and an example of his marvelous sense of showmanship.

But we had other ways of getting the goods on them. During séances we would break in on the spiritualistic discourse with a request that we be allowed to wash our hands or powder our noses. This being granted, we would retire to the lavatory and, unseen by the spiritist, would make a distinguishing mark, in crayon or chalk, under the bathtub or behind a mirror.

Then, when the séance had been resumed and concluded, we would pay the medium with inconspicuously marked money, and leave. Arrived back at our hotels, we would prepare a careful report for

Houdini. Provided with this ammunition, he would be all set for exposure on the following evening at the theater.

One of my colleagues was a young newspaperman, George Lait, son of Jack Lait, the short story writer, who was an intimate friend of Houdini. I have before me, as I write, two pages of George's personal memoranda, which contain the gist of my present theme.

"My reports," he wrote in his diary, "invariably contained not only the names and addresses of the mediums, but personal descriptions of them and accurate topographical charts of their séance chambers. I always made notations of the number on the bills with which I paid them, and included the exact hours of the séances, with precise collateral data.

$10,000 offer starts riot

"I also listed in the detail the questions I put to the spiritists and the answers which they gave. The particular forms of mediumship that they employed were also charted – trumpet–speaking, illusion creation, palmistry, mind–reading, ectoplastic evocations, or whatever it was.

The report would close with an indication of where I had left my mark on the premises. Fortified with this report, Houdini was able, usually, to expose the mediums without ever having seen them in person. In other instances, where they were extraordinarily wily and furtive, Houdini, in disguise, would pay calls on them, following the same procedure as his subordinates.

Invariably, when "turned up," the mediums would raise an indignant howl that their homes have never been entered by professional investigators, but the tell-tale chalk marks would disapprove this claim."

These excerpts from George Lait's notebook form a fitting prelude to the "big noise" that exploded when Houdini attempted to tear the veil from Mr. Slater's far–flung reputation. The occurrence – it is much too pale a term – was staged in Orchestra Hall. The place was packed. Human sardines; hot intensity; fervid expectation on the part of believers; loudly voiced skepticism on the part of the incredulous. The stage was set for fireworks and there ensued enough pyrotechnics to supply half a dozen Firsts of July.

Mr. Slater, as I have said, specialized in message reading. That is, he professed to be able to penetrate the meaning of questions sealed in envelopes and to give appropriate, informative answers. Houdini had given George Lait a certified check for $10,000 and had told him to challenge the medium on his public appearance before the vast audience.

"Tell him, "Houdini told George, "that I will bet this sum that I can reproduce by purely natural means any of the phenomena that he claims he produces supernaturally."

Thousands of times, literally, Houdini had before this duplicated the alleged "mystical" feats of other spiritualists.

Charity to benefit

In the case of Slater, the money at stake was to be donated, according to Houdini's terms, to a worthy charity – but this never came to pass, for reasons which I shall unfold.

George Lait, sensing possible trouble, took pains to be accompanied to Orchestra Hall by two friends. Bob Landry and Claude Binyon, of "Variety," whom he spotted in the house. I was seated inconspicuously in the rear and witnessed at first hand the ensuing scenes of panic, belligerence and flight on the part of many terrified persons.

Slater had started to do his stuff when young Lait entered into the house quietly and started towards the stage. But as he was about to leap over the runway, two roughs seized him from either side and tried to pinion his arms.

Infuriated, George broke away from them and, brandishing the $10,000 check in derisive defiance of Slater, again tried to reach the proscenium. Several members of the packed audience also grabbed him at that point, and he was forced to sit on the stage while Slater proceeded with his message–reading.

But the enforced silence began to get on Lait's nerves and, during a moment of total silence, he jumped to his feet and hoarsely shouted Houdini's challenge. Pandemonium followed. There was a wild and confused melee: one girl who had fainted had to be carried from the auditorium and there were innumerable small pitched battles between fervent and impulses spiritists and bellicose non-–believers.

George Lait, meanwhile, was shoved into the wings, and his coat was torn from his back. Before he could spring out of the way, a man struck him a glancing blow with a heavy mallet.

He finally however, managed to escape through the stage door. Re-entering the theater by the front door, he found the entire house in turmoil. The spiritists were madly applauding Slater, while the Houdini operatives, myself included, were booed and hissed. The demonstration broke up the meeting, Slater being unable to complete his manifestations of supernatural prowess.

Slater, despite his fame and his wealth, fared a little better in Philadelphia. Henry G. Hart, psychic investigator and journalist of high repute, wrote this about Slater's descent on the Quaker City:

"John Slater ... having boasted he would give $5000 to anyone who could prove his alleged communications from the dead are not genuine, hid ignominiously last night from Houdini as the magician offered to give $10,000 to charity if Slater would read five messages that he, Houdini, had written.

Slater is the cleverest message reader in or outside spiritism, yet at last night's meeting of the Pennsylvania State Spiritualist Association in Lu Lu Temple, he permitted the offices of that organization to prevent a fair investigation of his mediumship. He was fully aware that Houdini was in the audience.

The Pennsylvania State Spiritualist Association claims to harbor within its membership real mediums. At the meeting last night it refused to act to permit a reporter for the Record to introduce Houdini, and it refused to give to Mr. Slater a note requesting him to meet Houdini and permit him to accept the $5000 challenge offer.

Brawl on pavement

After the meeting a brawl occurred on the pavement outside Lu Lu Temple. Women engaged in fistfights, and cries of "fraud!" and "cheat!" we're directed both against Slater and Houdini. The millionaire medium kept within the inner recesses of the building. The crowd gathered about the automobile of the Reverend Mary H. M. Ellis, who was conveying Houdini downtown.

Yesterday afternoon Slater told the Record definitely that he had nothing to fear. He insisted that he was genuine, and, in the same breath, declared he didn't have to insist he was genuine. He then said he would give $5000 to anyone who could prove he wasn't genuine.

Houdini has frequently charged him with using trickery and subterfuge in reading the messages he claims are inspired by communication with the dead. Houdini has sent him registered letters inviting him to a test. He has offered to give $10,000 to charity if John Slater could read five messages that he, Houdini, wrote.

The moment Houdini entered, the word of his coming spread through the audience. Gilbert Armstrong, a second vice-president of the Association, immediately conveyed the news to the officers on the platform. Everyone knew Houdini was there. When a reporter asked for permission to speak and to introduce Houdini, it was refused and he was threatened with arrest."

Turmoil ends in fracas

The scenes of turmoil that ensued were similar to the fracas in Chicago, though they did not get so rough. Said Mr. Hart, in concluding his account of the affair:

"The readings he gave last night were on a par with the petty revelations of mediums exposed last winter... Slater hid from an encounter with the one man who can do what he does, but admits he does it by trickery. He sought and secured the protection of the Spiritualist Association. The Association still believes he is genuine."

And amazing and odd man, this Mr. Slater. Some of his ideas show a certain sharp–headedness; others, which she has gravely advanced in the press, are so curious as to be phenomenal.

"We have to rely on popular support," he once told a reporter. "There are plenty of rich people who have joined the spiritualists, but, if I may use the expression, they are a very stingy lot and I must admit that spiritualism makes them that way. It takes away the fear of hell and they are no longer afraid to die rich. They don't see the necessity of giving to save themselves from future punishment."

Slater also claimed that he had appeared before Keller, the great magician, and that the latter could not detect trickery. Sir Oliver Lodge and Camille Flammarion, the mystical astronomer, were cited as having given Slater a clean bill of health. I don't doubt it, but the "scientific investigations" of both men have all along shown a strong bias in favor of unsupported belief.

Speaking of psychic investigations, I will reproduce next week a rare old engraving depicting one of the earliest and most dramatic trials which took place in London in 1881. Toward the latter half of the 19th century, spiritualism had become such a rage among fashionable people of wealth that the police decided to take a hand. A woman named Mrs. Hart Davies brought an action against a Mrs. Willis Fetcher.

Capitalizes fraud charge

Mrs. Fetcher was required to stand trial in the Bow Street court for having, it was alleged, indulged in fraudulent practices. The accused woman, with great cunning, realized that whatever the verdict, the free publicity for her in connection with the case would be of inestimable value. She shrewdly capitalized this chance and her clientele increased by leaps and bounds.

Curiously enough, I can find no record of whether she was exonerated or convicted, but the chances are strongly in favor of the former, for England at that time was not equipped with the scientific means of "spook–baiting" that we possess today.

You will remember, perhaps, that in the Victorian era many persons of high literary standing were inclined to believe in the powers of spiritualists. Elizabeth Barrett Browning, for example, attended a séance given by an American spiritualist and appeared to be favorably impressed.

Her husband, Robert Browning, on the other hand, remained fairly skeptical and believed that the effect of séances on his wife's fragile physique was not good . You may look up his views on spiritualism in the poem, "Mr. Sludge, the Medium." The subject is "from the life."

Rose Mackenberg and the "Brocken Spectre" effect; a natural trick of mountain sunlight and shadow that can create the illusion of giant ghosts against clouds or mist.

Made in the USA
Monee, IL
25 October 2021